ditch the FEAR

&

Just Market It!

ditch the FEAR

&

Just Market It!

THE 90-DAY POWER PLAN TO ESTABLISH THE BOOK MARKETING FOUNDATION FOR BEGINNER & INTERMEDIATE LEVEL AUTHORS

Alexa Bigwarfe

Kat Biggie Press

Columbia, SC

Published by Kat Biggie Press.
Columbia, SC 29229
http://katbiggiepress.com

Cover design by Michelle Fairbanks
Interior customized and prepared by Write.Publish.Sell
www.writepublishsell.com
Licensed by Quick Wins Productivity System by Impact Stars, LLC

ISBN-13: 978-1-948604-81-9 (paperback)

ISBN-13 978-1-948604-82-6 (ebook)
Library of Congress Control Number: 2020910878
First Edition: June 2020

for all of the authors and marketing experts out there who have held my hand and taught me so much ... and to the authors who are dedicated to achieving success!

WELCOME

A Note to the Reader ... and some pre-work!

I am so grateful to you for getting this book and trusting me to help you market your book.

Welcome to what might be the hardest book you've ever bought!

I'm only half kidding.

But on a serious note, I need you to understand that marketing a book, ESPECIALLY your first book, when you are an unknown author, is HARD work. At the beginning, there will be a mega season of HUSTLE. For some of you, this season may be weeks. Months. For some of you, it may be years. This will vary based on genre, your level of marketing expertise, your willingness to invest in yourself or hire help to do this, how much time you have to work on it, and how seriously you take this process.

I've worked with a LOT of authors in the past decade, Indie/self-published, hybrid, and traditional. I run my own hybrid and traditional presses, but I LOVE to work with self-published authors, especially those who are willing to treat themselves like a business owner and take on the challenge of thinking like a publisher and a business owner.

What all of these authors have taught me is that you will have the most success if you take on that mindset of treating this as a business and treating yourself as a business owner, who is willing to invest in the tools and resources she needs for success.

Let's talk about mindset for a minute.

The reason my series of books for authors is called *Ditch the Fear!* is because there is a lot of fear, uncertainty, and mindset "stuff" that plays a role in all of this. (Don't try to deny it. I'm years into this stuff and I still have work to do in this area!) Most of us suffer from a variety of mindset issues when it comes to promoting our work. It's scary to put yourself out there, to be vulnerable. I talk about mindset right off the bat because we don't want your book marketing efforts to be stunted (or fail) because your mindset is stopping you from achieving more success.

As you become more educated about marketing and your confidence grows, you'll find that fear also goes away. If mindset is really plaguing you, especially as it pertains to your writing, I encourage you to get the first book in this series, *Ditch the Fear & Just Write It!* Although it helps writers get started with their first book, a big chunk of the book is about overcoming mindset issues and using affirmations to help you overcome any self-doubt you may face as a writer.

Before anything else, we establish the mindset base. Don't worry, we don't spend a lot of time there. Then we will move straight into a self-assessment of where you currently are, what type of marketing may suit you best, and work on creating a solid foundation. My work with hundreds of authors showed me that the biggest challenge new authors face is that they don't have the systems, processes, and foundations in place to build the audience (or readership) they need to result in the sales they wanted to see. So, I wrote a marketing book less about "marketing" per se, and a whole lot more on what you need to do to see RESULTS from your marketing dollars.

Who wants to spend tons of time and money on marketing that produces no results? NOT ME. I'm sure you don't want to either.

Because understanding your target audience (readers) is so incredibly important and worth many pages and exercises in this book, I want to start this welcome with a description of the target audience for this book.

Who is this book for?

The answer is not "everyone!" or even "all authors who want to market their book better!" I'd be breaking my own rules if I started out the book that way. One of the key rules of marketing is that you need to know WHO you are writing your book FOR in order to market it well.

This is a beginning to intermediate level resource on book marketing for authors. It is for the author serious about doing consistent work and taking the action steps to establish the foundation to grow their correct reader base, which will eventually result in more book sales. It's for the author who understands that there is no super special magical fairy dust that is sprinkled on your book when you put it on Amazon, resulting in magical sales. Sorry to burst your bubble, but you have to actually work REALLY hard, or REALLY smartly, to sell more books. Growing the CORRECT audience is the key to selling more books. And that's not always a simple task.

It's for the author who understands there must be some ownership interest. Advertising is not a nice-to-have for authors. It's a requirement. We'll talk about many ways to do that in a budget-friendly way, and how to leverage connections and opportunities to do so.

This book is for the author who is just getting started and needs some help creating their author platform and marketing strategy, OR for the author who is frustrated by the lack of results in their existing marketing efforts. If you are already selling a ton of books, you may not learn that much in this book.

More importantly, let's talk about who this book is NOT for.

This book is NOT for the author who only intends to publish one book. (It's not that I don't think you can't have success with just one book, but that is often a different route, a different type of author, like an entrepreneur who is writing a book primarily for business purposes to an existing audience. (This isn't the book for that person, although you might learn a thing or two.)

It is NOT for the author who will not commit to daily, weekly, and monthly activities to sell it. With the understanding that eventually, you won't have to hustle so hard, and your systems will do the work for you.

It is NOT for the person who is unwilling to make changes in what they've already done and learn some new tricks.

It is NOT for the person who is unwilling to invest time and money into their marketing efforts. The people who spend zero dollars marketing their book are also making zero sales. Unless they are famous. (And that is marketing in itself because they likely worked really hard to be famous.) Or they fit into the category of people who already have an audience.

This book is not like many book marketing books. For two reasons.

First, this book places a large emphasis on building the foundations so that when you start conducting different marketing tactics, you'll have greater success.

Second, it requires you to do work. Marketing anything takes work. If you do the work set forth for you in this book, you will see results.

But let me be clear. It takes consistent action and hard work, and sometimes the result does not show up for months. I repeat this message throughout the book, because it's important to remember!

Finally, this is the NO EXCUSES guide to getting your book marketed. I will ask you to do a lot of things in this book. If you want to see results, this is not a "read it and put it aside" book. This is an action-oriented power plan—filled with information and implementation steps. So, if you're ready to do this, you will have to ditch the fear, ditch the excuses, and remove expressions like, "I'm just too busy" from your vocabulary.

Throughout this power plan, you will find content about the topic at hand, some implementation steps or exercises, and examples and advice from successful authors who are lending their expertise to the lessons. It is my hope that these stories will resonate with you and show you that this is possible, even if you feel like the odds are against you.

If you're ready to challenge yourself, conquer some fears that may hold you back, be creative, review the work you've already done and consider if you might need to make some changes; if you're ready to take some action steps and do the work, I can guarantee you that in three to six months, you will have grown your audience, which will eventually produce more book sales.

Alexa Bigwarfe

Author, Author Coach, Publisher

CEO & Founder,

Write | Publish | Sell

Host, Women in Publishing Summit

Your marketing begins as soon as you have the following determined: a fleshed out idea for the book, an understanding of who the book is for, and an appreciation for the "norms" of your genre.

HOW TO USE THIS BOOK
building the foundation

This book was born out of the experience of working with many, many first-time and newer authors. I own three publishing imprints and work with self-publishing authors to prepare their books for publication, but I spend 90% of my time teaching our authors how to establish their author platform, develop their brand, set up their websites and social media ... and quite simply, learn the basics of marketing.

What became abundantly clear as we launched book after book is that many authors absolutely do not have the foundations in place that they need to effectively grow a platform and market a book.

Through many amazing book launches, we have learned a big secret about book sales. Numbers. It's a numbers game. You need high numbers of readers. (Not just high numbers of Facebook fans because you post silly memes, but people who want to buy your book.) That is truly the difference each time.

We could take the exact same book and launch it to different authors' audiences. One author, with an email list, an engaged social media presence, and a very clear target audience and another with no platform, no email list, and confusion on who they are trying to sell to. You can imagine who will have better results.

When you think about it, that's not rocket science. It's completely obvious. But it's surprisingly difficult to make a new author, who is in love with their book and believes it is the best book ever to hit the market (and it might be!), that just putting their book on Amazon and posting on Facebook is NOT enough to sell lots of copies.

I set this up as a 90-day power plan to build the foundation that you need to successfully market your book. It may take you significantly longer than 90 days or, you might knock this all out in two weeks, depending on your time and season of life, how much of this you can do on your own, and how much you have to take the time to learn before you can take action.

Each chapter should be about a week's worth of work. Don't be discouraged if you take longer! The important part is that you do the work and establish the solid foundation of your author platform.

Throughout this power plan, you will find content about the topic at hand, some implementation steps or exercises, and examples and advice from successful authors who are lending their expertise to the lessons. There is also a weekly goals check-in. Take the time each week to put together your goals, strategy, and the things you will accomplish. This can be as simple as searching key hashtags on Twitter and building your list, following and engaging with 100 new people on Instagram, or creating your lead magnet for your website.

The best way to reduce the overwhelm around marketing your book is to break it down into small, achievable chunks. My favorite commander, when I was in the active duty Air Force, used to remind me when I was overwhelmed that we eat an elephant one bite at a time.

Developing your author brand, author platform, creating and implementing your book marketing strategy over time is your elephant.

It is my hope that the case studies and input from the featured guest experts will resonate with you and show you that this is possible, even if you feel like the odds are against you.

Remember: this is the NO EXCUSES guide to getting your

book marketed. This is an action-oriented power plan—filled with information and implementation steps. But 'no excuses' does not mean you should suffer alone! If you need help, PLEASE come on over to the free Write|Publish|Sell Facebook group (https://facebook.com/groups/writepublishsell) and ask for help. Take advantage of the additional support we have set up for you (links throughout the book) and commit to doing this thoroughly.

The authors who put in the work will reap the rewards.

I'm excited to get started with you! Are you?

Next up: an overview of the tools and skills you need, plus some pre-work.

basic marketing skills

The most successful authors will have basic knowledge in the following areas:

- A true understanding of their target audience and how to get in front of them.
- A minimum level of understanding of how to be competitive in your market.
- The importance of networking and building relationships with readers, other authors, and other influencers, and how to get in front of them.
- How to grow your author platform.
- How to "market" as opposed to just spamming people with your book link.

More advanced skills that you should take the time to learn:

- How to communicate with your email list.
- Content creation - for blogs, social media, and so forth.
- How to run promos and stack them for more success.
- Advertising basics - Amazon Ads and Facebook ads, but these can be learned later or outsourced.

This book will teach you the first set of skills. The second set will be referenced, but not taught in depth. We have some additional support and extra resources for you to use at https://writepublishsell.com/JMI-secret. PW: JMIrocks

Tools

for your success

You don't need a lot to get started with your marketing, but there are some basic tools and skills that you should possess.

You will be best served to market yourself if you have the following minimum tools.

1. A website (even if super simple - but if you're really committed to selling more books, you need to be building your email list).

2. An email CRM (Convertkit, MailerLite, Mailchimp, Constant Contact, Aweber, etc).

3. A social media presence on at least 1-2 of the major social media sites.

4. A general book marketing strategy that includes pre-launch, launch, and post-launch long-term strategy.

5. A budget for marketing.

6. Most importantly: A good book, that's been well-edited, with a great cover and compelling description. And an understanding that understanding the READER is the most important tool for success.

There are obviously other things you'll need along the way, but these are the essentials.

If you don't have these already in place, I have set up some extra resources for you to use at https://writepublishsell.com/JMI-secret. Password: JMIrocks

PRE-WORK

commit to it!

Before we get started, there are a few things you should write down and commit to. Step one is to really make a commitment to creating a plan and implementing it, without giving up, even if it takes some time to see results.

Consistency is KEY. Until you are an author with a solid fan base (or are running a LOT of ads and marketing dollars to your books), the moment you stop actively marketing your book, the sales will stop. We've seen this numerous times—a book goes out the door strong and may have great sales for the first couple of weeks. And then ... nothing. A sale here or there. But are you content with low sales? You probably would not have bought this book if that were the case. As an indie author, marketing your book is now part of your job.

Make it a priority in your schedule to find time to implement the activities in this book and long-term marketing activities.

DETERMINE YOUR SCHEDULE

This should feel familiar. Just like you need to schedule time to write, you need to schedule time to market. My recommendation is to commit to 30 - 60 minutes / day or time blocking several hours in 1-2 days a week. In the beginning, you may want to set up more time and larger blocks while you establish the foundation of your marketing strategy. Beyond that, you may find that 15 minutes is enough on most days, with a larger block once or twice a week, depending on what phase of marketing you are in: pre-launch, launch, or post-launch.

MAKE YOUR COMMITMENT.

This may seem silly to you, but plenty of smart people say that _people who actually write down their goals are far more likely to stay committed and to achieve them._

I will commit to marketing _____ /minutes per day.

OR:

I commit to marketing these dates and times each week.

_____

_____

_____

OR:

I will block time on _____ days each week for my marketing implementation.

It really doesn't matter how you schedule it out, what matters is that you say, for example, "right now, I am committed to marketing and I will block one hour each day, Mon-Fri from 2-3pm EST for book marketing." Now go schedule this as appointments in your calendar and hold yourself accountable.

When you're starting out, I recommend you block 4-6 hours for initial market research, putting together your strategy and writing out your plan.

Before You Can Create A Marketing Strategy, You've Got to Have Goals

Successful book marketing strategies can be designed and achieved in so many different ways, but if you want to create a marketing strategy that will be effective for you, it has to be in line with achieving your goals. So, pre-work! Before you can do any marketing, it's time to set some realistic goals.

my crazy big goal (CBG)

What do I want?

Let's start with your really big goal. Why did you write your book? What are you trying to achieve? Are you building a business, starting a movement, or trying to become a professional author?

Is your goal to:

- Sell millions of copies?
- Achieve bestseller status? Become a New York Times bestseller?
- Make back any investment you've made so far in your self-publishing journey? If so, how much do you need to make from book sales to do so? And is this even feasible? (Is your book in a genre that is likely to make a lot of money, or should you consider other streams of revenue to support you?)
- Help someone change their life?

- Teach a skill?

- Grow your influence and credibility?

- Share your life lessons?

- Maybe you are far more focused on getting the book into the hands of the communities and organizations that need it than in actual sales numbers or royalties, and you'd like to focus marketing efforts on finding the inroads to your target reader?

These are all good goals. And all of them require a strategy that is based on achieving that particular goal.

WRITE DOWN YOUR GOALS.

First, what is your BIG goal? The big, hairy, audacious, goal, as some people say? The goal that terrifies you and yet excites you? Dreaming is okay but be realistic and set SMART goals. SMART stands for Specific, Measurable, Action-Oriented, Relevant, and Time Bound. SMART goals are more likely to be achieved.

Goal: Become a NY Times Bestseller.

That is a crazy big goal! And it is achievable... but it's not very SMART though. :-) The SMART version of this would look more like:

Spend 30 minutes per day working on connecting with readers and growing my email list so that I have the potential to achieve a major bestseller list within three years.

NY Times bestseller may not be your goal, but if it is, you need to make sure you figure out what is required to do so and set mini goals that will help you achieve that big goal. (The requirement, in case you're curious, is a minimum of 5,000 sales in one week and through multiple retailers. IE, not all 5,000+ sales can be on Amazon.)

Your turn. Think about it and write it down.

My crazy big goal is to:

Now the next part of this is setting smaller goals to help you achieve the big goal. Your marketing strategy should be based around the small action steps that you will take to achieve the daily, weekly, and monthly goals to get to the BIG goal.

SET MINI GOALS

SMART Goals

Specific, Measurable, Action-Oriented, Relevant & Time-Bound.

Think about the steps that are required to achieve your goal. Let's make our big goal - "Add 5,000 email subscribers to my list within one year by creating content that drives them to my website and encourages them to download my lead magnet."

Break BIG SMART goal down into daily and weekly chunks.

For example, there are 52 weeks in a year, 12 months. Perhaps consider a smaller goal of adding approximately 417 new subscribers a month, or about 96 new subscribers a week.

Right away, some of you might think that's too much and you may revisit your big goal. Or you might try to figure out what you need to do to hit 417 new subscribers a month.

Some other mini goals would be:

- Create a really good lead magnet / free download that people will want to sign up for.

- Begin running some ads to the download page.

- Look for virtual summits or conferences you can be a guest speaker at and gain new followers.

And so on.

Your turn.

Write some mini goals (what you need to get started toward the big goal, some weekly or monthly goals.)

I will _____

by _____(date) by doing _____.

I will _____

by _____(date) by doing _____.

I will _____

by _____(date) by doing _____.

chunk it up

BREAK IT DOWN

Use this space to write out more of your specific goals for the next 12 weeks.

BUT I JUST WANT TO WRITE.

You might already be thinking, Oh boy, what did I get myself into? I just want to spend my time writing! I know I am probably not the first to tell you this, but as an indie author, you signed up for the whole enchilada. And even traditionally published authors still bear the responsibility of some level of marketing and really need to know these skills if they want to sell their books. If you want to make a living as an author, you need to accept that part of the business of being an author is marketing. In the beginning it will be more time intensive. You have to lay the foundation and it takes a serious time and effort commitment. Eventually those actions will start to compound, and you'll find that marketing gets easier. As you get better at it, it will also become more fun. But marketing never stops.

Even well-known authors still have to participate in some level of marketing. Yes, it's likely that their publisher has a publicist handling all the groundwork, but they still have to make appearances and show up. James Patterson is one of the most famous and successful thriller authors there is. Yet he still shows up to promo events prior to launching a new book to sign copies and schmooze with his fans.

There seems to be a big misconception amongst many new authors that putting their book on Amazon will immediately make them a famous author. I am here to tell you that is not even a tiny bit true. Without solid marketing, your book will be quickly lost in the oca of millions of books. Marketing needs to be as important to you as writing your book. Think about this ... it's probably safe to say that almost every person in the developed world knows what McDonald's is ... or Coca-Cola. And they still pump millions of dollars into advertising each year. So why would you think you wouldn't need to also invest time and money into marketing your product and into advertising?

It doesn't have to be scary. If you're shy or introverted, there are tons of ways you can market your book without having to be interviewed live. At some point, you'll probably want to consider more publicity, but let's not lose track of our mission here. First, we must lay the foundation. We must understand the basics of marketing and what you need to do as a baseline to be successful.

A Note on Time & Budget

We are all busy. Most authors are on tight budgets. This is the NO EXCUSES plan. You've identified a problem with your marketing. You've invested in this book. Those are great steps forward. Now, invest in the time and figure out how to create at least a small budget for marketing. You don't have to spend thousands of dollars initially. You can bootstrap almost everything I teach in this book. However, at some point you may decide to hire people who are more skilled so that you can increase your book sales even more.

But for now, put aside excuses that you don't have time or money. Find the time. Do the work. Keep track of the wins and recognize your successes along the way. Most importantly, do not give up.

One Last Pre-Work Assignment:

Is Your Book Marketable?

This is a really important question to ask before you spend a lot of time, energy, and money trying to market a book. Sometimes we are entirely too close to our project and it's difficult to be objective.

The quality of the book, the quality of production, and how well you understand distribution go hand in hand with book marketing. It's important to acknowledge the fact that sometimes the problem with book sales is not the marketing. Sometimes the problem is the actual book itself. I know that hurts to read. But hear this: it's a solvable issue, 99% of the time.

IF you've been really struggling with sales, I highly encourage you to invest in a manuscript review and a cover review, and perhaps even hire a copywriter to work on your description. These reviews are not as expensive as one might think. Off the top of my head, Chanticleer Reviews offers manuscript evaluation, and I'm sure there are more companies that do this as well. These experts spend a lot of time and energy staying up to speed on industry standards and trends in the market. They also know what makes a good book. For a few hundred dollars, you could get some feedback though could completely turn things around for you. You'll need to be open to feedback and willing to make some changes if necessary.

Let me share an example of what I'm talking about. We recently published a children's book. We thought it looked gorgeous. The illustrations were incredible. The fonts were adorable. Until they weren't. We put it out for feedback and reader after reader reported that the font that we liked so much was difficult to read. Because of this feedback, we were able to change the font, and also make a couple of other changes that we were told would make the book more appealing for librarians in particular, before the book went on sale.

The same can be true with a plot that's lacking, a character that serves no purpose, or a self-help book that offers no real help.

It's difficult to see our own flaws. But sometimes the best marketing decision is to have the book assessed and make some tweaks to the book itself. I cannot express to you the importance of having a book that isn't "cringeworthy."

Other considerations that impact how the book is performing:

- Is it well positioned? IE, are the categories and keywords appropriate?
- Does the book fit well in the genre it's assigned?
- Is the book distributed / set up properly? Sometimes a tweak to the settings in IngramSpark, if you've distributed through that channel, can open up new doors as well.

So before doing anything else, ask yourself, is my book salable (yes, this is a real word, meaning 'fit to be sold') and positioned well? If you're not sure, this may be the best place to put your initial marketing budget and time. Please begin by filling out the pre-marketing book Self-Assessment.

The great news is that you can start building your marketing strategy and working on growing your platform even if you are putting your book through an assessment. Laissez les bons temps rouler!

Pre-Marketing Book Self-Assessment

Please answer each of these questions. If you answer NO or you do not know what one of these things mean, you've got some work to do to give your book the best chance at success. (If you're still writing your first book, keep this for when the book is completed.)

1. I have asked unbiased readers who would be the target market for the book to read and provide feedback and have implemented reasoable feedback. **Y / N**

2. My book has been professionally edited. **Y / N**

3. A print proof of my book has been proofread. **Y / N**

4. I have a professional cover design that is appropriate for my genre. **Y / N**

5. The book description / sales page copy is compelling and engaging. **Y / N**

6. My meta data is well-researched and appropriate for my book. **Y / N**

7. I have ensured that my book cover, copyright page, and other elements of the book meet industry standards*. **Y / N**

8. I have distributed (or am planning on distributing) the print book widely so that it is available for purchase by all retailers and libraries. **Y / N**

* The Independent Book Publishers Association (IBPA) has a free Industry Standards checklist on their website that will provide all of the information you need to ensure your book meets the minimum standards.

I JUST WANTED TO WRITE!

kirsten "kiki" oliphant

FICTION AUTHOR & PODCAST HOST

Kirsten Oliphant has her MFA in fiction and is the author of almost twenty books across genres. She is the host of the Create If Writing podcast, where she helps authors learn to sell more books without being smarmy. She lives in Houston with her husband, five kids, and Great Dane.

Kirsten has been hosting the Create If Writing podcast for five years and is a sought-after speaker. For several years running, she has been named one of Houston's Top 25 Social Media Power Influencers. She offers monthly paid workshops, coaching, and lots of free resources through her podcast, website, and free Facebook group.

Don't put limits on what you think you are capable of. Let yourself be surprised and amazing by what you can accomplish!

https://www.facebook.com/KirstenSOliphant
https://twitter.com/kikimojo

Genre: Fiction (Clean/Sweet Romance & YA)

Spend time learning your genre and studying amazon's categories. Really know the books that are doing well in your genre, get close to any of the authors that you can in Facebook groups to learn from them, and READ.

IF YOU WANT TO SELL LOTS, YOU HAVE TO KNOW WHAT IS SELLING

Kirsten is a big proponent on studying the market to determine what readers want to buy. She said, "I would be much more clear about knowing the market before putting out a book. I would base my decisions on what sells, not what I like." It took her a little while to see what was really happening within her genre, but she set to work to know, understand, and conquer the Sweet/Clean Romance genre. There are so many subtleties at play with these genres that Kirsten writes under several pen names so that she doesn't confuse her readers.

It took a few months of really writing, marketing, and hanging out in the online space alongside other authors for her to realize where she was making missteps and how to clarify her efforts. She continues to learn because the environment continues to evolve.

Kirsten shared that her biggest struggle was mindset. She wanted to write books and have them sell and she didn't want to focus her time on marketing and selling. She just wanted to be a creative. Once she realized that marketing is really just connecting with her ideal readers, things became a lot easier and way more fun.

She quickly realized that if she was going to be successful, she had to take on a business mindset and spend the time to treat her writing career and publishing as a business. It was hard starting out with no money, bootstrapping everything from covers to ads and learning the entire process along the way. And this is one of the main reasons that she turned to studying the market so that she could ensure her hard earned efforts would pay off. And it has, indeed, resulted in great rewards.

Kirsten's full can be found at https://writepublishsell.com/just-market-it-featured/.

To learn more about Kirsten, her books, and her podcast, please visit https://www.createifwriting.com.

1-Mindset

MORE THAN JUST FEAR

Congratulations on making your commitment and setting some goals. That's a big step! Did any of them scare you? Do your goals make you nervous? Do you have a hard time believing that you are a New York Times bestselling author?

For the lucky few, mindset and fear are not issues. But for many authors (especially women!), these fears can keep us from moving forward at all. Common fears for authors circle around fear of rejection, not wanting to talk about themselves in front of people, fear of the reaction to their book (negative feedback) or to them as an author (why is SHE writing that book?). And there's also a fear of investing a lot of money in tactics that don't work. Or how about fears that no one will show up or buy your book if you schedule an author signing or event at bookstores or libraries? And of course, being afraid that no matter what you do, your sales will not reflect your effort.

It doesn't matter how consistently you are working towards implementing a strategy, it's still really demotivating if the results aren't immediately obvious. You should be prepared that if you're starting with no email list and little to no followers / reader base, you are unlikely to see giant results quickly. I repeat this message throughout the book, because it's important to remember so that you stay on track and stay motivated to do the work! But when you feel like you're spinning your wheels and getting no traction, you may want to give up.

I've interviewed a lot of authors along the way. Most of them did not see any traction on their marketing efforts for at least three to six months with their first book, (and some much longer than that!) unless they'd already done the work to build their audience before launching. And almost all of them struggled with self-doubt because of this. But they kept at it and eventually pushed through. Mind over matter.

When it comes to book marketing, another giant mindset issue can be the feelings of utter defeat when you are not getting results; launching a book and not seeing sales. Or not getting reviews despite repeatedly asking your friends and family to go review the book. I urge you to keep taking consistent action EVEN when you're scared that you're failing, you aren't good enough, your book isn't good enough. If you've done the pre-work and you're confident that you have a good book that is professional and high quality, then it's far more likely the issue is not your book, it's that not enough of the right people know about it.

Fears are completely common issues and I want you to know even the most successful people struggle with this. But if you let the fear guide you, it will cripple you. Before you take action, always ask yourself: What is the WORST thing that can happen? For authors, you might get some negative reviews. Or sales might be lower than you hoped for. You might not make the money back you invested. But the best-case scenario? People love your books, you get great reviews, and once you've got the numbers on track, you're seeing great sales! Is it worth not getting to that result because of fear?

I am not a mindset coach per se, but I DO know struggles well. We have so many limiting beliefs, so many fears, so many internal blocks that can really slow us down from achieving our goal of making a living as a writer. The answer to these fears is practice and consistent effort.

If you need any inspiration on this at all, you should read about some of the journeys of super famous athletes. They discuss how hard they tried, how much they practiced, how many shots they missed on the journey to be a great athlete. Why would we think that we as authors would not also have to do some work?

Not only on our craft, but work on our marketing, positioning, and even, books that people actually want to buy and tell all their friends about?

So, it's time to stop focusing on the bad stuff because **those thoughts will not serve you.**

There are some other considerations with relation to mindset. Mindset is not just about fear and the things that hold us back.

Mindset is also about how you approach your book marketing.

Are you setting yourself up for failure with unrealistic expectations?

Are you being honest with yourself? This is important. Are you telling yourself that you just want to sell your book to family and friends so that you aren't disappointed that no one else is buying? To be clear, it's PERFECTLY FINE to write a book that you only intend for your family and friends. And if that's your goal, then you don't necessarily have to invest in marketing and all of those other things. But you DO have to make sure that you will truly only be happy with that as your outcome.

Approach book marketing as a hobby, and hobby results you shall see.

But don't let fear be the reason you decide this is only a little project for friends and family.

Your mindset can also be impacted by some ingrained beliefs and misunderstandings. These mindset issues center around your expectations, your beliefs about what you need to do, to pay, and what the outcomes will be. There are some pretty prevalent myths that many authors hold dear that contribute to authors not taking certain actions that would potentially be good for them.

Let's talk about some of these myths.

Myth 1: I'm a self-published author. I should never have to pay anyone to help me publish my book.

Myth 2: I want to be traditionally published and I won't have to do my own marketing.

Myth 3: I don't need to pay for advertising and marketing.

Myth 4: My book is going to sell tons of copies just because I've done the work to launch it well.

Myth 5: I wrote a great book in a popular genre, so it's going to sell tons of copies.

Myth 6: I can publish my book first and market later. (oh dear.)

Myth 7: I have a lot of friends and family who will buy my books. (Nope.)

If you're a hard-core DIY'er, and you've subscribed to the belief that you should never pay anyone to help you or you can do all of your marketing on your own, this can be problematic when it comes to seeing big results. Despite what some people will tell you, you do NOT have to do everything on your own to be an indie author. And you MUST invest in your marketing. At some point you have to pay for things. Even if it's website hosting and the annual fee for your email CRM, there will be expenses. If you're truly going to see high sales, you're also going to have to do some advertising.

For those seeking traditional publishers, you'll need to overcome any idea that you don't have to do this work because you have a publisher. You might get launch support, but after that, you're largely on your own.

While you CAN take the route of waiting to market until you're done writing and it IS possible to do all post-launch marketing, you will miss some exciting opportunities. We've also found that the work is harder post launch than pre-launch, especially if it's going to be a long time until you launch another book. I'll talk about this in the chapter about thinking like a publisher.

For those authors who believe all you truly want to do is sell some books to your friends and family, you don't necessarily have to invest in marketing and all of those other things to build a big audience. BUT: if you take this route, you DO have to make sure that you will truly only be happy with very low book sales as the outcome.

At this juncture you may want to revisit your goals and make sure that your goals are on track with your expectations and that your expectations are realistic.

Now that we've talked about different types of mindset issues you may face, I want you to spend a moment thinking about any fears, objections to marketing, things that have held you back, or myths that you have bought into. Maybe it's a myth I didn't include.

WRITE THOSE DOWN HERE:

After you've written down the fears, objections, and myths, review the goals you set in the prework. I want you to cross out all these fears and I want you to GIVE YOURSELF PERMISSION TO SUCCEED. Write the following statement:

I will not allow fears, objections, or myths to stop me from achieving my goal of (write your goal). I give myself permission to be a marketing beast.

If you've got a lot of mindset issues surrounding marketing, you may need to start every marketing session by repeating that statement.

Now it's time to infuse our brains with **positive ideas**.

Instead of fears, let's focus on our dreams. Our dreams are different from our goals because these are the things that our wildest imagination craves.

dream big!
MARKETING SUCCESS IS COMING TO ME.

Give yourself five minutes to write down all the dreams you have for what could happen with your books and your author career.

Weekly Goals

At the end of each chapter, and in preparation for the upcoming week,I include a weekly goals check-in. This is a reminder for you to write down the goals and hold yourself accountable.

First, consider if there are things you have to do before you can work toward that goal.

For example, if you want to work on building followers on Instagram, do you need to set up your Instagram account? Or perhaps you need to work on the bio section to make sure that when people do land on your IG account, they know who they are following.

This should not be a "shame" list. IE, if you don't get to some of the tasks or accomplish a goal one week, you can transfer it forward to the next. But *pay close attention* if there are any tasks or goals that you continuously avoid. These may be areas that you either need more training on or might consider hiring help to accomplish, especially if they are significant milestones for a larger goal.

I suggest that the first few weeks should be all about the topics of the chapter you've just completed.

Also—It's okay to get help!

Weekly goals _____

Set aside at least 20 minutes at the start of each week to plan for the week. Specifically, when will you be working on marketing & what do you want to achieve?

My goal for the week is:

_____

_____

_____

Is there anything I need to do before I can work on this goal?

_____

_____

_____

On a scale of 1-10, how committed am I to achieving this one goal this week? 1 2 3 4 5 6 7 8 9 10

My baseline: (keep track of where you started this week. This will be based on your goals. So if it's social media growth, how many followers do you have today? If it's book sales or reviews, what is your starting number?)

_____

_____

_____

MISTAKES WERE MADE – AND LEARNED FROM!

angela applewhite

ROMANTIC SUSPENSE AUTHOR

Angela Applewhite earned her BA in English and Professional Writing from the University of Waterloo in Waterloo Ontario. She spent most her professional life working in law and technology. Angela is an indie author who published her first novel, *Torn: A Forensic Romance* in 2018 after 8 years of thoroughly researching the book. Her second book, *Twist of Fate*, published May 7, 2020. Her third novel, *Compromised Daughter*, is forthcoming. She lives in Toronto with her husband and daughter.

> *"Our scars make us know that our past was for real."*
> *Jane Austen*

https://www.facebook.com/readapplewhite
https://twitter.com/readapplewhite

Genre: Fiction (Romantic Suspense)

I shied away from booking an official in-store signing because I didn't think I had enough traction to generate interest. I worried that I would just sit there and no one would buy the book and I would be crushed. By the time I built the nerve to book a date, all the dates were taken. Don't let your fears hold you back from achieving success!

LEARN FROM YOUR MISTAKES

Angela published her first book, *Torn: A Forensic Romance* in November 2018. On the 23rd the book went live with no marketing plan, no email list, and no idea that it was already on the market; she'd forgotten to change the launch date on IngramSpark! The wrong version went live. (No judgement here, we've done this as well!)

Angela was worried about what her blunder would do to the book sales, but she was really confident in her book itself, which had a beautiful book cover, designed by Jessica Bell.

Angela really wanted to see her book in the local brick and mortar stores. When she contacted the manager of acquisitions, she realized she'd made a few other rookie publishing mistakes. He pointed out to Angela that *Torn* was set up with Ingram was 'short discount' (36% to retailers and not-returnable), she would only be able to get the book into stores using consignment. He suggested a wholesale discount of 55% and including the USD and CAD prices. He also informed her that she would need to send an outline of her (non-existent) marketing plan to the regional buying manager for Central and Eastern Canada. A quick learner, Angela did just that and she was able to get her books in the store.

Even though Angela made mistakes and had fears, she kept working at it. She experimented with some Facebook ads for traffic, sought out editorial reviews, joined some coordinated promo opportunities, and more. And despite her blunders, lack of a marketing plan, and no mailing list, she saw decent sales after about the first three months.

As more time has passed, Angela has continued to invest in her marketing, through hiring different agencies and paying for courses to improve her knowledge. You can see all of her marketing efforts and her full interview here: https://writepublishsell.com/just-market-it-featured/.

BIGGEST STRUGGLES:

Angela admitted her biggest struggles in marketing are not having a sizeable mailing list, not knowing where or how to find her audience, and figuring out which 'marketers' were there to help and which ones were taking advantage.

One thing is clear, even though Angela struggled with some mindset issues and some setbacks, she has continued to learn, to implement, and to tweak her strategy. She's still working to see the big, huge results, but she's getting better marketing every day. This is what it takes to be a successful book marketer.

To learn more about Angela and her books, please visit https://applewhite.ca

CHAPTER 2

The Foundation

We can't become what we need to be by remaining

where we are.

~ Oprah Winfrey

Unless you are already trained in marketing from some other experience, you probably don't actually know much about marketing a book. Don't be offended by that statement. It's a normal starting place. I didn't feel like I truly knew how to market a book until we had multiple launches under our belt. It's likely that you might have some training in book launch strategies, or have attended some webinars or summits and courses, but it's probably more likely that so far much of your marketing has been piecemeal and is not based on a strategy or any type of foundation.

If that's your situation, you are normal! Most of the authors I work with have spent all their time writing and revising their book, and don't realize until they are ready to publish that they should have started building an audience and started marketing MONTHS ago. Just as your craft of writing will improve the more you write, your marketing skills will also improve as you learn more and implement. The key is making sure that you're learning and implementing the RIGHT strategies and tactics that will work for your book, your genre, your readers, and your marketing ability and comfort level.

Marketing anything takes work. It can be challenging and frustrating and feel like it is yielding little to no results in the beginning. It's even more frustrating when you feel like your marketing efforts are like throwing spaghetti at the wall. Do you have a plan? A budget? A timeline? Do you know who you are marketing TO? Do you understand the analytics and data to know if your marketing efforts are successful or not? Is your email list and fan base growing?

Backing even farther up, do you even understand what "marketing" means? That may seem like a stupid question, but there are some people who think marketing their book consists in nothing more than putting it on Amazon and sharing the link on their Facebook page.

Many first time authors have no idea about most of the above. But through trial and error, we begin to get our education. Sometimes this can be very costly, but we learn through our mistakes. Which is fantastic because you can make some massive improvements by not doing what didn't work the last time. But it can also be really frustrating.

I want to tell you a story about my second book because that's where all of my marketing lessons were learned. My first book, I didn't do much marketing for (or at least, I didn't recognize the marketing) because it was a passion project and I just desperately wanted any grieving mother who needed my book to have it. I didn't care about selling it. I gave (and still give) it for free to anyone who needs it.

But my second book, *Lose the Cape! Realities for Busy Modern Moms & Strategies to Survive* is an amazing case study in marketing failure. Let me just list out all the mistakes we made.

- We assumed that because we were mom bloggers and writing a book for moms that every mom (ever!) would want to buy this book.

- We assumed that since we interviewed a ton of moms for the book that they would want to buy the book (and share about it!) - wrong.

- We assumed that since it was co-authored and both of us had our own tiny little platforms and lots of friends and family that we would sell a lot of books.

- We figured we could market it once we had the book published and make up for lost ground, and therefore did no pre-launch marketing.

- We thought our mom blogger community would line right up to buy and share about the book.

- We thought 100 advanced readers would result in tons of promo and reviews and sales.

- We thought just having the book on Amazon would generate sales.

- We didn't understand that book retailers will not buy books to sell in their stores from Amazon and expanded distribution does not really mean expanded distribution.

Many mistakes were made. And they all boil down to one central theme: we did not understand marketing, launches, saleability, or even our own target audience.

In the feedback from our advanced readers, who didn't understand the importance of leaving their review on Amazon in addition to posting on social and their blogs (which we were also grateful for), we learned that our target audience was actually new moms.

After receiving multiple praises that read something like: "Wow, I wish this book had been around ten years ago when I had my first child!" or "This is such a fantastic book for the new mom!" or "You should buy this book for the next baby shower you attend!" we began to realize that we, in fact, did not understand our target market at all. We should have been marketing it alongside the What to Expect When Expecting crowd or anyone writing to brand new or pregnant moms. Instead, we were spending all of our time trying to get it in front of established moms.

We also did not do nearly enough in terms of building up our audience, building fans who eagerly anticipated the book, or prepping for the book launch. Now I know the error of my ways.

An example on the complete opposite side of the spectrum is a now very famous hilarious mom blogger (not a mommy blogger, but a mom who blogs) who used Facebook to create hilarious videos as she wrote about her story of being arrested for drug use, went to jail and rehab, and is now raising a family as a recovered addict. She shared her story, grew her audience, built her fan base, and when she published her book (which by the way, she blogged almost the entire thing over the course of a couple of years), the book sold a bazillion copies and she had over 300 reviews in the first couple of weeks after her launch.

This is the difference in building the RIGHT audience, knowing who that is and how to capture their attention, and creating a fan base of people that adore you so much that they will buy the book even if they read almost the entire thing for free on your blog.

She created the foundation for success. She was focused. She set her mind to growing that audience and did it in such a fun and creative way that her people are loyal. They buy everything she tells them to buy, which makes her a dream "influencer" for brands.

Not everyone is going to have that kind of success. Even if I wanted to, I couldn't produce the funny videos that she does or in the way she does it. And not everyone has years to build their base before they publish their book. So don't be frustrated and think that you can never make that happen.

Instead, you have to lay the foundation of success by understanding WHO will buy your book, HOW to get in front of that audience, WHAT are the ways and the channels to get in front of them, and WHICH marketing tactics are going to be comfortable and successful for you. If you are TERRIFIED of speaking in front of live audiences, by all means, you should not pursue speaking events as your primary tactic, or doing live video presentations. At least not at the beginning, but you should always strive to stretch and try new things, little by little.

In most situations*** you will have to figure out a way that you feel comfortable being at least slightly in the public eye. But this can be through podcast interviews (which are pre-recorded and off camera) or guest writing opportunities—blogging, writing articles, submitting to digital and print publications, contributing to other content, participating in author events and workshops or on panels, signing and giving away copies of your books at industry events, book retailers or library events, or networking in other ways that will grow your fan base.

*** There are always exceptions to every rule, but the biggest exception are authors who are publishing books so prolifically that they have a tremendous back-list, in a genre like romance where some voracious readers are reading a book or more per DAY, and those that are pumping a ton of dollars into advertising. Since that situation probably doesn't apply to the people reading this book, we'll assume you need to do the work to build your fan base.

There is a great article written by Kevin Kelly called 1000 True Fans. The concept is that you don't need millions of people following you to be successful, you need 1000 TRUE fans, that will buy everything you ever sell. They have bought in. The problem with this theory for authors is that you need more than 1000 sales, even if you have lots of books. BUT, the best part about readers who are true fans is that they talk about your books. They tell others when people ask for recommendations, and sometimes even when they don't. In the past week alone, I've had four girlfriends reach out to me via text and ask me if I've read "insert title" yet. Most of the books had been suggested to me by multiple people at this point. So the glory of true fans is that they help you build a follower of more true fans.

But it doesn't happen overnight. And it most certainly doesn't happen by chance. It is strategy and implementation. Work.

My favorite example of a false "overnight success" is the story of E.L. James. While you may not recognize her name, you probably recognize the title of her book. She wrote *50 Shades of Grey*. Many people like to herald her as an overnight success. They are wrong. Check out the chapter on Building Your Platform for more details on what happened with this situation.

If you do the work, especially if you spend the time to create a solid marketing plan and implement it, you will see results.

Your book marketing foundation is built on some key elements:

- Understanding the business of being an author, in particular thinking of yourself as a publisher and behaving as a publisher would.

- Creating and implementing a strategy based on realistic goals & marketing tactics that are comfortable and realistic for YOU to implement.

- A well-defined target audience

- An author platform that is centered on building an email list.

- Consistent effort, which begins long before you launch, into launch, and long after the book is published.

- Paying attention to the results and tweaking the plan if necessary.

If you do the work, especially if you spend the time to create a solid marketing plan and implement it, you will see results. This "work" is centered around three main foundational steps.

Step 1 is to take the time to understand the publishing

industry and think like a publisher, which includes truly studying and understanding the market for your book.

Step 2 is to spend the time to figure out who your target audience is and how to get in front of them. Learn and know your reader.

Step 3 is to create a plan that has goals, milestones, and objectives for marketing your book beginning early in the publishing & launch process. The most important part about the strategy is that it needs to be filled with actions that you are comfortable and willing to take and directed at the correct target audience. Finally, it needs to be implemented consistently over time.

The rest of the book will be information, exercises, and action steps for you to take to be able to build this foundation.

When To Start Marketing

You start marketing when you understand who your READER is, if you want to be the most successful. And early in the process.

So your initial "marketing" per se, is learning to figure out who that reader is, and make sure everything you do is inline with what the reader would want or is interested in.

While there are many parts of launching and marketing a book that are fairly generically effective across the board, there is also going to be a lot of the strategy that is personal to you. Just remember, while strategy is important to overall success, you can build your strategy along the way, but you can never make up for time lost. Start early! Start now!

I am probably going to repeat this 1000 times in this book. Because it is a question we get asked over and over and over and over and over and... you get the point.

Now! Yesterday! 6 months ago!

Basically, I think the moment you get serious about writing a book, you should start "marketing" it. And I think this crosses all genres and all routes to publishing. Because even IF you get picked up by a traditional press, it will never hurt you to have a larger audience.

Now, there are varying levels of marketing, right? But as we just went over, there is a TON of foundational work to be done - in terms of audience building and target audience development and building your email list, etc.

So start early and do the things a little bit at a time that will help you build as you get going.

Even if you don't have a cover, a book, free chapters to share, or anything.

Here's what you CAN do while you are writing your book:

1. Start finding groups, forums, fanfic sites, and other places that are talking about your genre. These can be authors, readers, reviewers, anything, but you'll want to start making connections and learning from other people.

2. Start the process of setting up your website and your email and all of that fun stuff.

3. Work on your branding. Set up social media.

4. Blog, guest post, or find other ways to start talking about the topic you're writing about. This is super easy for nonfiction. For fiction writers, the easiest thing to do to start getting attention from other readers who are into that genre is to start posting book reviews on books in your genre. You can do these on social media, on your blog, on a podcast, on YouTube, on Goodreads, or on many of the other sites you can find.

5. Spend REAL time digging into your market and comp title research. You should read at least ten of the bestselling books in your genre. More depending on the genre. Less maybe for some.

6. Connect, connect, connect. The biggest secret to marketing, my friends, is that it is largely about building relationships and making connections. And then authentically serving and providing value to the READER that will want your book.

Fun story about me and my marketing. I write almost all nonfiction but I want to be a novelist so badly. I LOVE World War 2 historical fiction books set in Europe. About three years ago, I decided I was going to write one. I outlined the book in my head (I'm a pantser!) and decided on the general plot. I decided the title. *Angel of the Burning Night.* And I emailed my cover designer and started asking her to work up some concepts based on my idea.

I set up a launch group, invited all my friends and family, and put a landing page on my website.

To that point, I had not written one.single.word of the book. I now have about 60,000 words of a crappy first draft that desperately needs more research and revision, and I'm working slowly through the process. That book probably won't be done until about 2025, and by goodness, I will have a massive following built up by then!

So it's never too soon to start marketing. You cannot make up for the time that it takes to make all of these things happen. But you WILL be best served by making sure you have done the work of audience development first.

If you're already done with your book, I strongly encourage you to give a solid three months of giving away the book, building your launch team, getting reviewers, and so forth before you launch.

Weekly goals _____

Set aside at least 20 minutes at the start of each week to plan for the week. Specifically, when will you be working on marketing & what do you want to achieve?

My goal for the week is:

_____

_____

_____

Is there anything I need to do before I can work on this goal?

_____

_____

_____

On a scale of 1-10, how committed am I to achieving this one goal this week? 1 2 3 4 5 6 7 8 9 10

My baseline: (keep track of where you started this week. This will be based on your goals. So if it's social media growth, how many followers do you have today? If it's book sales or reviews, what is your starting number?)

_____

_____

CONSISTENT EFFORT WILL PAY OFF

annalisa parent

WRITING & PUBLISHING COACH

Annalisa Parent helps writers to finish, publish and sell their novels. She owns and operates Date with the Muse, LLC, which helps storytellers to publish traditionally at the highest level possible. A magna cum laude graduate of Middlebury College's English Department & Creative Writing program, Parent studied writing under Julia Alvarez and Jay Parini. Her first poem was published when she was 10 years old, and she was selected to read it aloud at a ceremony in the state house of her home state of New Hampshire. More recently, she and her award-winning book Storytelling for Pantsers: How to Outline and Revise your Novel without an Outline were featured on four segments of Creative Life with Sheryl Borden on PBS.

Writers write. (As in, it's that simple.)

https://twitter.com/annalisaparent

Genre: Nonfiction

It takes a while to get your name out into the marketplace. When you're "nobody" at the beginning, it can feel like you're constantly speaking into the void. These are the moments when showing up and staying consistent are difficut.

STAY PERSISTENT

Annalisa shared that understanding your target audience and showing up in front of them regularly is really important. Persistence is key.

"Show up everyday. Do the facebook live when no one's watching. Tweet into the empty void. Keep on keepin' on. Oh yeah, and provide VALUE to your audience. No one wants to hear about me me me or Buy my book. Be someone you'd like to hang out with--and people will come hang out with you."

But Annalisa warns to be true to yourself in the process. People love authenticity and it's important to just be you. Your "fans" will appreciate it.

Annalisa Parent helps fiction writers to publish and sell their books. She offers a free consultation at www.datewiththemuse.com/publishnow.

CHAPTER 3

Publishing is a Business

Part of creating your foundation for success as an author is embracing the publishing business. If you've chosen to indie publish your book, you've also made the decision to be a publishing expert. If that's not what you want, you may want to consider hybrid publishing or even seeking out a traditional publisher. Because as an indie author, you wear all the hats. Writer, project manager, creative director, marketing manager, and so on and so forth. And to be successful, you're going to want to be familiar with the business.

Yes, you can (and should!) absolutely hire publishing partners to help you with the fine details of editing, cover design, layout. But even with those key elements handled by pros, you still have to possess the knowledge of how to position your book, what the industry standards are, what the norms of your genre are, and what your readers want to see.

Think like a publisher.

What does that mean exactly? Well, it means that when you're thinking about publishing a book, you're thinking about the book as a product. You are building a business around your book. In addition to your marketing strategy, you'll probably want to consider creating an author business plan. You need a budget and a timeframe and goals. Other things a publisher knows: categorization and BISAC codes, keywords, pricing, Imprint names, and so forth. These are things you now have to be the expert on. Additionally, you want to learn as much as you can about industry standards (be sure to check out the Industry Standards checklist, downloadable on the Independent Book Publishers Association—IBPA).

All of that is a bit too much for us to delve into for the purpose of this book, and there is so much of a knowledge base here that it will take time and experience to truly know all of these things. And truthfully, you can be successful without knowing EVERY detail of how the publishing industry works. But you need to know YOUR niche, your genre, the area of the market you are trying to conquer. So it's worth becoming as educated as you can. I encourage you to start thinking about these things. Are you treating yourself like a publisher and a business owner or do you simply think of yourself as a writer? You may find you approach many things differently once you have accepted the fact that you are more than just a writer. You're a small business owner.

Thinking like a publisher also means understanding ROI, or the Return on Investment for the marketing strategies you employ. It certainly means understanding you may not see an ROI for some time, depending on the strategy in play.

I get this question a lot. If I hire you to do (x service), will I sell more books? If I pay for a blog tour, will I see book sales? If I pay to enter an awards program, will I sell more books? If I pay for editorial reviews, will it make that much of a difference?

The next part of thinking like a publisher is in timelines for publishing.

So many authors get so excited about finishing their book and want to publish it ASAP! They don't understand the LONG game strategy that requires building the audience first, launching strong, and building from that. You miss out on so many opportunities when you rush to launch.

There is a very good reason why traditional publishing takes so long. Yes, writing and editing takes time. But most books published by a large house are marketed for a year prior to the 'on sale' date. While that may seem excessive, you should at least give yourself a solid three months to build up hype from the type your book is in final format until publishing.

We prefer 6 months if not 9 for our authors.

Bring Your Network On Board Early

I'll say it again. Allow for plenty of time to market your book and grow your reader base. From the publisher perspective, this means creating opportunities to get in front of new audiences. In this case, we're considering events, putting your book up onto sites like Netgalley to get more eyes on from book retailers, librarians, and avid reviewers, and lining up publicity of an assorted manner.

What activities do you do in that time? So many things.

- Attend events
- Build your launch team
- Send your book to reviewers
- Guest blog, get on podcasts
- Run a media campaign.
- Put out a press release.
- Seek out editorial reviews.
- Build buzz.

Attend bookseller or publishing conferences or industry events, first as an observer so you can learn. You will see stall after stall of authors giving away copies of their book. And most of those books won't even be published for another quarter or more from that time.

While you do not likely have the budget to print 10,000 advanced reader copies and travel to multiple major industry events, there are ways that you can still get your book into the hands of many readers with enough time for them to actually read, review, tweet about, share about, and spread your book around so that people are looking for it.

Even famous authors are still getting out and hyping their books before they come out. I met James Patterson at the Book Expo America in 2017 and Charlaine Harris (author of the True Blood series) at a regional bookseller's conference in Spartanburg, SC in 2019.

If you were working with a large to medium-sized publishing house, you would likely be assigned to a Publicist. This person would arrange for author events, author signings, interviews, and all of those things to get your book and you as the author in front of a wide audience. Publicists can be very pricey, so this may be something that you decide to hire out, or you can even search for people in the industry who offer courses on the subjects, like Kristi Dosh, who has a publicity and PR course that was created specifically to authors who need help in this area. As we've established, the most successful book launches are those in which a LOT of people have already heard about and seen the book everywhere.

If attending events is not feasible or comfortable, use your time, energy, and funds to grow a strong launch team. I encourage my clients to set up a launch team from very early on in the process. If you've just started writing your book, it may feel scary to even think about sharing details of your book, but it's amazing how much support you can get from a launch team, which will keep you motivated. The best part is that you can start a launch team while you're in the process of writing your book.

The launch team is comprised of the people that will be your biggest cheerleaders throughout the process. You can create a community (like a group on Facebook, or a special email list) where you keep them updated on your progress. Let them be part of the process—they can help you pick your title, your cover design, encourage you when you're feeling stressed, help you brainstorm when you feel stuck, answer polls and surveys when you need input or feedback. They'll love being a part of your book launch! If you're further along in the process, start where you are. It's never too early to start talking about your book!

CONTINUE TO LEARN

More than just stepping out for visibility, industry events are exceptionally educational as well. Continuing education and professional development are crucial to your growth as an author entrepreneur. Imagine if doctors and nurses never did any additional training or education after they received their education. Even if you have an MFA, that still does not prepare you for all the knowledge you need to successfully run a business as an author.

Some of the best resources for improving your knowledge of the industry (which WILL result in doing things better) are the Independent Book Publishers Association (IBPA), the Author's Guild, the Alliance of Independent Authors (ALLi), associations like Publisher's Weekly, Writer's Digest, the American Booksellers Association (ABA), the American Library Association (ALA), and regional organizations and any organization specific to your genre, like the Society of Children's Book Writers and Illustrators, the Romance Writers of America, or the Nonfiction Writers Association, and so forth. Google resources for writers, resources for publishers, and then get genre specific. There are many out there providing so much excellent education for those who are serious about increasing their knowledge base.

Beyond publishing and marketing more of your own books and taking the time to become educated, a great way to learn a lot about the industry is by researching the competition. Not just any competition, but the competition that is performing well. You can do this by visiting retail sites or going into bookstores and truly studying the books that are the best sellers in your genre or your category. You'll want to look at the covers, the descriptions, where they are placed, the main category, the subcategories. How are they priced? Tools like PublisherRocket and KDSpy can also give great insight into how much the book is selling each month.

You might not be able to hop in your car and go to your local bookstore right now, but you can go on Amazon and look at the best sellers in your category.

The important part is that you step out of your Author Avatar and think about your marketing efforts as if you were running a Publishing house. This will help you position your book better and be more successful in your book marketing efforts. The following exercise will help you learn the tools to not only position your book for success, but also grow your understanding of your genre through examining what is working well for other authors.

Think Like A Publisher - Study the Comps

otesica johnson

STORY TELLING STRATEGIST

Otescia R. Johnson is a bestselling author, screenwriter, success coach, publisher, and international keynote speaker. She holds a Bachelor of Science degree in Business Administration and uses her education and background in the business world to manage her companies; B.O.Y. Publications, B.O.Y. Enterprises, & O. Johnson Ministries. Otescia is the author of 12 published books and several screenplays. She is also the creator of the Magnetize Your Life system, the Publisher Partner Academy, and the Broke to Profitable Success Coaching Program. When she isn't writing and inspiring others, Otescia can be found enjoying life with her husband, children, and grandchildren.

The greatest question any writer can ever ask is, "What if?"

https://www.facebook.com/BetOnYourselfEnt
https://twitter.com/BetOnYourselfEnt

Genre: Fiction & Nonfiction

My biggest struggles as a new author were not understanding how important marketing is to the success of a book, and mistaking social media posts as a marketing campaign. I didn't know anything about mailing lists or how to nurture subscribers.

Study Others in Your Genre!

Are you seeing this as a recurring theme yet? To succeed as an author is to know the business of being an author. This holds true whether you are self-published or traditionally published.

Otescia shared that one of her tips for success is to think like a publisher so that you can position the book well. You do this by researching successful books in the genre in which you are writing. Study keywords, sales page info, meta data, reader reviews, and anything else you can find on the top 10 books in the genre in which you are writing.

Once you have all of that information, you can create a plan to align your book with those that are already successful.

Otescia shared her best advice is for new authors. She said, "Be creative. Marketing is not about being the one who talks the most. It's about being the one who is *saying something in a way the consumer has not heard before*. Can you speak from a point of view your target audience seldom hears from? Can you share little known statistical data? Can you touch the pain point of your target audience with the first line of your sales copy? if you can do those things, you can sell anything."

This is particularly good advice for anyone writing in really competitive genres - say, shape shifting fantasy or health and wellness. People still want to read more of those subjects, but how is yours different than the last book they read? And how is it the same? Some things need to be consistent within the genre. If you study the genre, you'll come to understand the subtleties of figuring out which things you model, and where you want to distinguish yourself.

Read all of her advice and full interview at: https://writepublishsell. com/just-market-it-featured/

Learn more about Otescia at: http://www.betonyourselfent.com

Smart Positioning
How to Get Your Book Out There

Proper positioning of your book is one of the most important skills you should learn as quickly as possible.

What does positioning it mean? It means getting your book(s) in front of the CORRECT audience and visible in the places where that audience is most likely to see it. It means creating a lot of buzz and growing your author platform. It means getting the book in front of as many of those people as possible and finding a way to capture those people as your fans.

Smart positioning means knowing and understanding your genre and what the expectations are of the genre. What books are selling well? What are the trends? How do you properly price the book? What is normal for covers, as an example, and does yours fit in the genre you've selected. Do you have the appropriate keywords and categories? Is the description similar to other books? It's understanding how to find the other books that are similar and ensuring readers who love those books will also find your book appealing.

So how do you smartly position your book(s) in a way that creates buzz in an authentic way that promotes audience growth and more book sales? I'm about to show you, and then you're going to do it.

Exercise
STUDYING YOUR GENRE

This exercise is to show you how to learn as much as you can about the genre you are publishing in to help you position your book most successfully.

Here are the step by step instructions followed by an example. I encourage you to read the entire exercise before you start to implement on your own.

STEPS

1. Go to Amazon.com or your favorite online retailer (as long as they list books by rankings and show key data.)

2. Search the genre + best sellers

3. Click on one of the books that looks most interesting to you.

4. On the sales page, navigate down to the Product Details and look at the Amazon Best sellers ranking.

5. Click on one of the categories.
    You will be taken to the top 50 best selling books in that category. Look at the whole page and pick the 5 that stand out most to you.

6. Click into each book and really study them.

7. Open up a blank word document or Google Doc, save it as "Key data on comp titles" and collect the following data:

- Book title & author

- URL to the Amazon page (so you can revisit the link later)

- What stands out about the cover?

- Does the cover have some similarities to other best sellers in that genre? Similar fonts, color schemes, et?

- Study the description. Even copy and paste the description to help you craft yours similarly.

- Write down the categories it is ranking in. Be sure to click into all formats of the book. (ie, the Kindle categories might be different from the paperback, which may be different from audio.)

- Notice if there are any keywords in the title, subtitle, and description. How do you know this? Look to see if you can find the same word in either the title, subtitle, and repeated in the description. Sometimes they are not that obvious.

- Look at the pricing on all formats.

- Look at the publisher. Is this obviously traditionally published or indie?

8. Read the reviews. They are chock full of information.

While you are collecting the data, follow the authors. If you have time, check out their bios and websites, and also follow them on social. You might even want to see if you can find their contact information to ask them for an endorsement blurb or another collaborative effort later. Save this as a task for another day if you don't have time to go through with the author research today. Repeat this for 5-10 books. I assure you, you'll learn some things.

BONUS TIP: if you aren't reading the best sellers in your genre, you need to get on it! Check them out through the library ebook or audiobook program and read, read, read.

Example

My genre is historical fiction. I opened Amazon and typed into the Amazon search bar: "historical fiction…" and best sellers self-populated. I chose that. As it happens, my specific area of interest is World War 2 books set in Europe, even more specifically, France.

The book that popped up at the top is All the Ways We Said Goodbye. A book about World War 2 set in Paris. It is ranking in World War 1 books, Women's domestic life, and World War 2 books. Kindle also has an historical fiction WW2 category.

I noticed that the hardcover book is ranking much higher in the categories than the paperback version. This makes sense. Since most indie authors do not do hardcover format, there are far fewer books competing in the category. It's ranking top 100 in hardcover and in the hundreds or thousands in paperback.

I also noticed that the covers of the books in this genre are very, very similar. So similar that I first thought I had already read this book until I read the description. You might think this is a bad thing. However, from a reader's perspective, psychologically what happened in my mind was an almost instant desire to add it to my cart because I knew how much I enjoyed the other books I have read in the genre.

Being different is not always a good thing. At least not with the covers. Yes, you want a storyline that is different from the other million books in the category, but you want your readers to trust that your book fits in the category, in the genre, and will fit well in their reading list.

After reading the description and taking notes on that, I read reviews. Reviews are an incredible piece of information for you. It's got a lot of great reviews from people that enjoyed the story. People who are really into the accuracy of the historical aspect were not as enamored, and were sure to point out the inaccuracies. (A key detail when writing historical fiction is knowing if the technology you describe actually existed at that time!)

Negative reviews can be so helpful because it teaches you some really key insights. First, many people who love books about this time-frame love the stories of spying and resistance. One negative review pointed out that this is not what you'll get at all. This is helpful knowledge about the genre and reader's of this genre, and can be useful in the description of the book. Good reviews are also helpful when they describe what the readers really liked. You can use snippets of reviews on your own books to further enhance the description of your book, too.

If you want to really practice how to write a great description, take it to the next step and type out the sales page description of each book so that you train your brain to think in the same formula.

I credit this tactic to the amazing Brooke Warner, CEO of She Writes Press, memoir expert, and writing coach. She was my first coach and she told me if I wanted to write like some of the greats in my genre, I could practice those skills by typing passages from their books. (Never to steal or use anywhere! Simply to train your brain to write words like great writers do.)

OK, time to get to work. Of all the exercises in this book, this is likely going to be the most helpful to you. The more best selling books you study in your genre, the better you are going to be at positioning your own book and ensuring that your book fits with the expectations of the readers in the genre.

Upon Completing the Exercise...

Now that you've completed that, you're well on your way to understanding how to position your book.

As we discussed earlier, the other key element of thinking like a publisher is in setting the timeline for publishing. Do you have a good idea for how long the editing and production of your book will take? Have you made sure to account for PLENTY of time to market the book once you have a final copy to share with advanced readers and influencers?

So many authors get so excited about finishing their book and want to publish it ASAP! They don't understand the LONG GAME strategy that requires building the audience first, launching strong, and building from that. You miss out on so many opportunities when you rush to launch.

Don't be that person. Give yourself time. I know you're excited to get that first book out there. But guess what? You can put it on pre-order if you're worried about losing sales during your marketing. Your launch will be so much more successful because you took the time to establish your foundation in your marketing.

Weekly goals _____

Set aside at least 20 minutes at the start of each week to plan for the week. Specifically, when will you be working on marketing & what do you want to achieve?

My goal for the week is:

_____

_____

_____

Is there anything I need to do before I can work on this goal?

_____

_____

_____

On a scale of 1-10, how committed am I to achieving this one goal this week?
1 2 3 4 5 6 7 8 9 10

My baseline: (keep track of where you started this week. This will be based on your goals. So if it's social media growth, how many followers do you have today? If it's book sales or reviews, what is your starting number?)

_____

_____

_____

Position Yourself to Be Where You Will Be Found!

shayla raquel

EDITOR, BRANDING & MARKETING EXPERT

An expert editor, best-selling author, and book marketer, Shayla Raquel works one-on-one with authors and businesses. She has edited over 400 books and has launched several Amazon best sellers for her clients. Her award-winning blog teaches new and established authors how to write, publish, and market their books. She is the author of the Pre-Publishing Checklist, "The Rotting" (in Shivers in the Night), The Suicide Tree, and The 10 Commandments of Author Branding.

"Impossible is just a big word thrown around by small men who find it easier to live in the world they've been given, than to explore the power they have to change it. Impossible is not a fact. It's an opinion. Impossible is not a declaration. It's a dare. Impossible is potential. Impossible is temporary. Impossible is nothing." Muhammad Ali

https://www.facebook.com/shaylaraquel/
https://twitter.com/shaylaleeraquel

Genre: Fiction & Nonfiction

Practice authenticity first and foremost. It is the foundation of everything you will do when marketing your book and branding yourself as an author. If you aren't yourself, then you're wasting your time.

Show Up in the Right Way

Shayla struggled with target marketing. When she started blogging, she was directing her posts at editors. However, she realized if she was going to draw the right audience to her website, she needed to be writing to new authors.

She came to this realization after she hired a brand marketer in late 2014. He pointed this information out to her and she was able to adjust her copywriting and position herself as someone who was there to help authors hold their books in their hands, not someone writing to help editors.

Shayla recommends everyone should work with a brand marketer. Just the small shifts that she made because of his advice resulted in a 35% profit increase.

When it comes to positioning the book for the correct target audience, Shayle recommends that you *spend the time learning to truly understand where your book will get the most visibility and engagement is to understand what problem your book solves and where people "hang out" with those problems.*

For example, if your book is targeted toward Gen X-ers who are reentering the workforce now that their kids are more grown up, get on LinkedIn and write helpful articles on the topic. If your book is targeted toward Millennials who want to get in shape, then post 1-minute videos on Instagram to teach them simple ways to improve their health. Solve their problems!

Learn more from Shayla here:

Blog: https://shaylaraquel.com/blog

Book: https://shaylaraquel.com/10commandments

How-to videos: https://shaylaraquel.com/howtovideos

These are also some of my favorite books on writing, marketing, and the like: https://shaylaraquel.com/shaylas-picks

CHAPTER 4

Finding Your Target Audience

Your Target Audience.

Have you put much thought into the actual people that want to read your book?

That might seem like an asinine question to some of you, but you'd be surprised how many authors NEVER think about their target audience until they go for help when their book isn't selling.

This is the meat of the book, dear readers, and we're going to spend a LOT of time here.

You may be surprised to know that many authors NEVER think about their target audience until they go for help when their book isn't selling. Or, they assume they know and understand their target market so well, they don't think they need to spend a lot of time here. Until they realize they may know their audience, but they aren't quite sure how to get in front of them.

For example, an author may assume that because they've written a romance novel, readers who like romance will just love their book. But when there are 4 million (I just made that number up but it's probably not too far off!) romance books on Amazon, how on earth do people find YOURS?

Understanding your reader is one of the most important elements of the book marketing process.

The target audience is going to vary greatly by genre.

If you don't know WHO you are writing your book for, how do

you know it's solving the pain point (nonfiction) or meeting the genre expectations (fiction) of the norms that are to be expected. Yes, readers have expectations of what will happen in the genre they love to read.

We'll dig into the differences between the audiences for fiction and nonfiction in the exercise below.

Knowing WHO you are marketing to makes everything about marketing easier. The clearer you can get about the likes and dislikes of that person makes it easier to create content that will be interesting to them, to talk in ways that will be appealing, and to know where to show up and how to position yourself and your book(s).

First, let's see who you BELIEVE your ideal reader is right now.

EXERCISE 1:

WHO I THINK MY IDEAL READER IS:

Who is your ideal audience? Who are the people that will want to read your book? Use this space to jot down notes about your reader.

* * * * *

After you've taken the time to write down what you believe your ideal reader is, it's time to do a deep dive into finding out if that is true or not, or if there's anything you're missing that could enhance your ability to market to her.

Now that you have described this person, do you feel comfortable in being able to figure out how to show up in front of them? Or do you need to spend more time further defining this persona?

I think you'll find that as you start to do the research, it's not always so clear. Even if determining your audience is simple, it can still be challenging to get your book in front of them.

This is where a solid foundation combined with a strategy that is consistent and appropriate for your genre and your audience come together.

Over the next several pages, we're going to cover:

- Why understanding your target audience is so important
- Complete an exercise to determine your audience

- Discuss some ways to get in front of the audience
- Talk about ways to incorporate this into the marketing strategy you'll be developing

WHY IS IT CRITICAL TO UNDERSTAND YOUR AUDIENCE?

Let's just establish the fact now that every marketing tactic you do is easier when you know WHO you are talking to. The clearer you can get about the likes and dislikes of that person makes it easier to create content that will be interesting to them, to talk in ways that will be appealing, and to know where to show up and how to position yourself and your book(s).

HOW DO I FIND THE RIGHT PEOPLE?

You can approach this from several different ways. First, look at other books that are similar to the book you are writing. Twitter has an advanced search function that allows you to enter in key words and phrases and see who is talking about what. Use this to see what people are talking about the authors who have written books similar to yours. https://twitter.com/search-advanced.

Research which keywords are trending. Google Trends will show you how popular certain terms are. Enter a generic keyword in your niche, such as "romance novel,", and see the interest over time and also what related queries are most frequently used. This will help you see what terms are trending and what keywords are useful for you, both in your research and for your book meta data.

If you already have an established audience, send out a poll or collect feedback directly from your current readers. You might be surprised what they have to say about what interests them and what does not.

Your task: Create a reader persona. Knowing this level of detail can help you look for groups and forums on Facebook, LinkedIn,

Twitter, and other places where you may be able to connect with and attract fans.

Be sure to include key details like:

- Who are they?
- What do they like?
- What do they like to read & why?
- Where do they hang out (social media, online, physical places)
- Why would my book appeal to them?

UNDERSTANDING THE TARGET AUDIENCE BY GENRE:

FICTION

The audiences for fiction books are largely based on the genre and the subgenres. For fiction, understanding your target audience comes down to knowing what they like about a certain genre and why. It's about understanding their expectations as a reader and even more importantly, understanding where you're going to disappoint them.

When you can really hone in on the likes and dislikes of readers, it makes everything easier. Experienced authors in the fiction genre will advise you to be a reader of that genre you are writing in, so that you know exactly what the readers want. Clean romance readers, for example, are averse to sex scenes in a book. Everything down to the picture on the book cover should send a signal to them that this is safe, what they expect, and even if you take it a little steamy, there will be no sex. Probably no curse words either. If you put foul language and sex in a book you market to clean readers, you will get skewered. These are the types of details that are important to know about your target audience.

NONFICTION

On the nonfiction side, it can be a little easier to determine. If you're writing a vegan cookbook, the audience is pretty clear. At least at first glance. But then you can break it down further by determining if this is a person who is new to being a vegan and if they need additional information in the book, or if this is to people who have been vegan for years and want no extra fluff, just new recipes. While the positioning for publishing is not too difficult to figure out, your messaging is going to be different based on the audience within that genre.

Not so complicated, right? You'd be surprised. Because once you figure out who wants to read your books, you have to learn how to sell to them.

Maybe you're thinking, this will be a piece of cake! My audience is comprised of voracious readers, and they'll buy everything in the genre. (This is me when it comes to books by Brene Brown or anything about WW2 set in France!) Even if that is true, if you haven't written a book that meets your audiences expectations, they will tear you to shreds, and that will end your credibility in that genre.

What problem are you solving for them? And then get really specific about it. The "problem" may simply be that they love reading books about Presidents. So you're solving that problem by adding another book for them. Or it could be that they really want to learn how to meditate and have no idea how... Think about what they want to learn from the book.

When possible, get really specific and include things like:

- Gender
- Personality
- Family life
- Job

- Location
- Needs
- Pain points
- Challenges

You might wonder why we are getting so detailed. You may or may not need all of this information, especially fiction authors or children's book authors. Nonfiction authors that are likely trying to sell something other than books really do need to dig deep. The better you know the person, the better you will understand their interests. The better you know their interests, the more likely your marketing efforts will be successful.

OTHER WAYS YOU CAN DISCOVER WHAT YOUR TARGET AUDIENCE LIKES OR WANTS:

- Website data. Make sure you have Google Analytics installed on your website. This will provide all kinds of great information to you, like what keywords they are using when they come to your site, demographic information, actions they take.

- Spend time in forums and groups and read/engage in discussions.

- Read reviews of the other books in your genre. Study your comp titles!

- Talk to other authors in your genre.

- Poll your existing audience. If you already have an established audience, send out a poll or collect feedback directly from your current readers. You might be surprised what they have to say about what interests them and what does not.

- Review social media analytics. If you already have a Facebook Author or Business page, you can look at the Facebook analytics for information on how people are engaging with content you're already putting out plus you can monitor similar pages. You can view the insights and click on the PEOPLE tab to see some details about the types of people that are following or interacting with your page.

- Social media data: Twitter and Instagram (and most social media tools) have an advanced search function that allows you to enter in key words and phrases and see who is talking about what. Use this to see what people are talking about the authors who have written books similar to yours. https://twitter.com/search-advanced.

- Research which keywords are trending. Google Trends will show you how popular certain terms are. Enter a generic keyword in your niche, such as "romance novel,", and see the interest over time and also what related queries are most frequently used. This will help you see what terms are trending and what keywords are useful for you, both in your research and for your book metadata.

EXERCISE 2:

CREATE A DETAILED AVATAR FOR YOUR IDEAL READER

Now that you've learned a bit more about how to do the research, you can spend a bit more time creating a full 'persona' for your reader. An Avatar is just a fancy name for a really detailed description about a person.

Things you should not do when building your customer Persona:

1. Assume they are just like you
2. Assume they know the same things as you

Once you have created your "avatar" for your ideal reader, every time you write a blog post, an email, a social media post, write it as if you are talking to that one specific person.

My Ideal Reader Is: (Avatar)

Use this space to jot down notes about your reader. Make the description super clear. Name her if you want. Then every time you write a blog post, a social media post, an email, you can think about "Suzie Q" as you do so. What would she want to read? What would interest her?

Even Experienced Authors Struggle

I interviewed 16 authors and book marketing experts for this book. I wanted to know if determining and understanding the target audience was a universal struggle because knowing who your target reader / audience is plays such a critical role in your success at marketing your book. I asked all of the guest experts the following question:

How long did it take you to really understand your target audience / ideal reader?

Almost everyone answered that it was more complex than they thought it would be. Here are some of their responses:

Amy Collins: "Once I started to research? 3 hours. But it took me 5 years to stop ASSUMING I KNEW my readers and actually DO the research."

Mel Storm, who has hit the NY Times Bestseller list with multiple books answered: "I'm still learning about my readers, and I'm always researching to try to get better in touch with them. There are still times where risks I take don't pan out, so it's constantly a learning experience. Things really clicked around 2008, the same time I started venturing out and attending industry conferences. That's a great way to force yourself to learn how to explain your work in tight, powerful sentences!"

Na'ima B. Robert: "Several years as a fiction author."

Kirsten Oliphant: "It took a few months of really writing, marketing, and hanging out in the online space alongside other authors to realize where I was making missteps and how to clarify my efforts. I'm still learning! And the market continues to evolve."

Angela Applewhite: "I'm still learning. I still have to figure out what excites them and entices them to buy."

Angela J. Ford gave some insight into why this is tricky, even when you already know and understand the audience. "I am my own ideal audience. I read fantasy and I write fantasy, I usually buy ebooks on Amazon, I'm enrolled in Kindle Unlimited and I'm a part of several groups where I can discuss books and get recommendations. While understanding my target audience was key, I had to work hard at making my books visible to them."

Eva Natiello: "My first book is a psychological thriller and I knew that they are always on the hunt for the next thrilling read. I had a great list of comp books which helped me direct my marketing efforts." Comp titles can really help you understand what your audience is looking for as well.

Kasie Whitener: "Weirdly, one of my earliest beta readers told me who my target market was back in 2015. I should have then cultivated that market, but I don't think I knew what to say to them. Even now, I doubt how many of us there are. Rebels, irreverent, a little dirty, the "like mes" out there have been hiding their true colors for a long time."

What can you take away from this?

Determining the target audience and how to market to them is a problem that many authors face. The sooner you can get to work to find their audience and set up the proper marketing strategy for them, the better of you'll be.

Want to read more from our guest experts? You can find all of the full interviews and all of their books here: https://writepublishsell.com/just-market-it-featured/

Cautionary tale

I observe many authors who spend too much time hanging around in author groups and NOT spending the time developing the relationship with the people who actually want to read the book. Other authors can be tremendously important to your growth and the journey. But they are not going to buy your book. So while you should definitely use groups for writers as a way to build relationships and possible areas of collaboration, helping each other promote each others' books, etc, it is NOT the place you should be trying to sell your book.

I'm going to try to be as gentle as possible here, but I need you to understand - other authors are NOT and will NEVER be the target audience for your book.

For example, I run the Facebook Group Write|Publish|Sell (https://www.facebook.com/groups/WritePublishSell/).

Our goal is to provide resources to help authors write, publish, and sell their books better, as well as to foster a community of writers and service providers where we can share resources, get help, and get support. But it never fails, there's always someone who comes and posts about their book all the time. I can assure you, if you're doing this, you are wasting your time. Because they aren't coming to this group to buy books. Even if your book looks like one that might interest them. This tactic does NOT work.

What DOES work is getting in front of the people who are looking for and want your book and providing value to them. This value comes in a variety of sizes and shapes, and is going to be largely dependent on what your target audience wants and needs.

Is it entertainment? Is it solving a problem? Is it learning something? These are the questions you need to answer to understand your target audience, and it will vary heavily by genre.

It's not that complicated. We tend to over complicate it, but first and foremost, put yourself in the mindset of a reader.

In Summary:

Readers are the people who will buy, review, and recommend your book. They are the people you need to find and cultivate a relationship with. That doesn't have to be a deep relationship, but they need to feel like they know you well enough or receive enough value from you that they open your emails, engage on your social media, and buy your books.

Marketing Task!

Have you already set up a landing page to start collecting email addresses? This is a relatively simple way to get started.

Action Step

Set up a landing page or a form on your website with a call to action for people to get on your email list.

If you have a book you can give away for free, use that.

If not, come up with something that is RELEVANT to the target audience of your book. IE, if you're writing a book on Yoga, don't give them a free download of your favorite Vegan Recipes. If you're writing a sweet romance, don't give them a short story about werewolves.

Be sure to connect it properly to your email CRM and work on having at least a couple of emails in a nurture sequence so they can get to know you better and what you/your book is all about.

If you have absolutely no idea how to do this, I highly suggest my blogging 101 course for authors, which has several modules dedicated to setting up your website and your landing page and connecting it to your email CRM. Learn more here: https://writepublishsell.thinkific.com/courses/blogging-101.

I'll even give you a 25% discount code for being a book buyer! Thank you! Use the coupon code **jmirocks**.

It doesn't have to be complicationed. But now that you've done the work of identifying your target audience / readers are, you'll be able to start building a list of THOSE people, not just a random list who will not be interested in reading or buying your book.

Weekly goals _____

Set aside at least 20 minutes at the start of each week to plan for the week. Specifically, when will you be working on marketing & what do you want to achieve?

My goal for the week is:

_____

_____

_____

Is there anything I need to do before I can work on this goal?

_____

_____

_____

On a scale of 1-10, how committed am I to achieving this one goal this week? 1 2 3 4 5 6 7 8 9 10

My baseline: (keep track of where you started this week. This will be based on your goals. So if it's social media growth, how many followers do you have today? If it's book sales or reviews, what is your starting number?)

_____

_____

_____

Start Marketing Early & Consistently

eva natiello

NEW YORK TIMES BESTSELLING THRILLER AUTHOR

Eva Lesko Natiello is the NEW YORK TIMES and USA TODAY bestselling author of THE MEMORY BOX, a self-published psychological thriller which has sold hundreds of thousands of copies worldwide. She is a sought after speaker and has appeared at ThrillerFest, BookBaby Independent Author Conferences, Morristown Festival of Books, Liberty States Fiction Writers Conference, Women In Publishing Summit, among others. Eva draws on her 20+ years of experience in PR, marketing and branding to coach authors on self-publishing and book marketing. She is the creator and facilitator of Self-Publish Like a Pro and Find Your Readers Book Marketing Workshops. Her next thriller is forthcoming.

"If you want to go fast, go alone. If you want to go far, go together."
African Proverb

https://www.facebook.com/EvaNatiello
https://twitter.com/EvaNatiello

Genre: Fiction (Psychological Thriller)

I understood my ideal reader right away. My first book is a psychological thriller and I knew that they are always on the hunt for the next thrilling read. I had a great list of comp books which helped me direct my marketing efforts.

MARKET EARLY TO YOUR TARGET READER

Understanding your target audience is so critical to indie authors. Eva states that her biggest struggle was getting her book noticed. When you self-publish a book, you don't have a PR team, Sales team or Marketing team. She had to figure out how to leverage the benefits of being an indie to create visibility for my book.

Because she understood her genre and the norms of her genre, ie, what the reader wants in that genre, Eva was able to learn a lot from studying comp titles. (Do you see a theme here?)

Eva says, "If you don't know where to position your book, create a list of comp titles (books that are comparable to yours) and look to see how they have positioned theirs." When in doubt, follow the direction of the people who are having success!

Eva admitted that doing this work was not a lot of fun for her. Studying the comps and the market was the one chore (besides writing a synopsis for her book) that she dreaded doing. She admitted that at the time, she didn't realize all the benefits a list of books similar to her book would provide. Especially for marketing.

Eva's advice for authors looking to grow their audience is to become a rock star within your own community by starting your marketing efforts on the local level. In her interview for the Women in Publishing Summit, she talked about going out to her local beaches and handing out marketing materials and having a great time creating a buzz.

She also advises to make sure your book is as professional looking as possible. Appearances are everything. Starting with your book cover, through to your retail sales pages and continuing on to your website and social media pages. Make sure they are professional to attract readers and boost sales.

To learn more about Eva and her books and marketing services for authors, please visit https://evaleskonatiello.com.

CHAPTER 5

Build Your Strategy

Good long-term marketing requires some sort of strategy behind it. Yes, you can just throw spaghetti at the wall and see what sticks, but you'll be better served by actually having some sort of plan, tracking what you're doing and the results those activities have.

You'll want to have a plan for audience growth prior to launch, your launch window, and then post-launch marketing.

Developing a full marketing strategy takes a lot of time and effort. It requires a full understanding of the channels available to you as well as an understanding of what you are capable of accomplishing.

This is key. YOU have to be willing/able to do the work or to pay someone to do it for you. So if it's going to be you, make sure you focus on doing things that you feel comfortable implementing.

There are several main areas you'll want to focus on to increase sales.

1. Author platform - hands down the best way to sell more books is to have a bigger, dedicated audience. Your number one priority should be in growing your author platform - primarily through the growth of your email list. Your platform consists of your email list, your social media influence, and the places that people go to follow you or engage with you.

2. Visibility - higher visibility will naturally help you grow your author platform. You may greatly increase visibility through using influencer tours; leveraging other people's platforms to shine a light on your work. Think about podcast appearances, guest blogging opportunities, interviews on summits and other programs, creating your own content on your blog, participating in group giveaways or book marketing bundles and other activities. Visibility also includes understanding how to properly place your book with keywords and categories. If you aren't positioned properly, you will not be found by organic traffic alone.

3. Paid marketing - promo lists, Amazon ads, Facebook Ads, other paid marketing strategies for authors. All of these are fantastic ways to increase sales but usually require a pretty good level of knowledge on using them properly and effectively.

Before you can create your strategy, you should identify as many places as possible where you can show up. I call these the different marketing channels, and we'll cover those in a later chapter in more detail. But awareness of the channels and when it is most effective to utilize them will help you develop a time-based, goal-based strategy for guest appearances, etc.

Understanding your Own Marketing Avatar/ Profile

As we dig into strategy, it's important that you do NOT freak out about the things that make you uncomfortable. Not everyone wants to be on podcasts, summits, or other interviews.

The best marketing strategy is going to be a solid combination of all 3 of the areas mentioned above, used in conjunction with each other for max visibility, but you do not have to do them exactly as prescribed or exactly how others are doing their marketing.

QUICK NOTE: Simply because an idea is suggested in this book does not mean it is the ONLY way to do something or that it is mandatory for success. I assure you, there are many different ways to achieve success, and some authors have sold tons of books without being very public. The trade-off is that you have to spend the money elsewhere. So if you don't want to do the work to put yourself in front of readers, then you basically have to pay to let advertising channels do that for you.

Additionally, you should never be comparing what you are capable of doing and achieving with what other authors are doing, especially if they are a successful author or entrepreneur who has been around for a long time. As much as I would like to launch a book like Brené Brown, that would be a ridiculous comparison. For goodness' sake, she hangs out with Oprah! She probably has a million people on her email list, she has a full-time staff of people doing all the heavy lifting, and it's just a completely unrealistic comparison. So I need to base my marketing strategies around the goals and objectives that are realistic considering my experience level, my budget, my support team, my email list, and my overall audience size.

So, in the popular words of the day, "You do YOU." Just do it smartly and based on a legit marketing strategy. If you aren't comfortable doing speaking, interviews, and live events, you need to brainstorm some ways you can get in front of other audiences without doing this. I encourage guest blogging and articles for journals and websites, newsletter swaps, and so on.

But do me a favor and promise me you'll try to learn and stretch yourself to do things outside of your comfort zone.

For those of you who know me as the host of the Women in Publishing Summit, constantly conducting interviews, both live and pre-recorded, and running workshops, it may surprise you to know that I used to be TERRIFIED of speaking in public. And ironically, I chose the career path as a professional briefer in the military. I had no idea when I chose my Air Force career field as an Intelligence Officer that I would actually have to stand in front of audiences (sometimes of hundreds of people) EVERY DAY and provide information. There were many embarrassing incidents, but eventually, I became a pro. Surprisingly, I began to really enjoy speaking in front of people, especially about topics I love. So, I believe you can become comfortable doing things that scare you too. And the best time to practice is when you have a small fan base.

Creating Your Strategy

Let's start with a reality check. *Marketing strategy is not something creatives are gifted with just KNOWING.* Any kind of strategy takes a lot of work and understanding of the marketplace and the behavior of buyers, in addition to knowledge about how to put together a plan that works together but is also measurable. I can teach you some basic action steps that will be to the benefit of pretty much every author trying to build an audience, but the information will be very general. As part of your growth and development, you need to invest the time in learning the other part. Studying your comp titles and your genre will help you do this.

There are several different ways to create a marketing strategy. You'll want to include the big goals you are trying to achieve, and then break it down into the milestones and activities you need to take to get there. Each part of the strategy can be broken down into tasks, resources, things you can do on your own, and things you might want to hire others to do for you.

At this point, I suggest you open up a word or google doc, title it "Marketing Strategy for BOOK TITLE" and begin typing it all out.

I like to see the following things included in a marketing strategy:

1. An overview of the key book information.

Include key metadata - title, description, keywords categories

Include your comp titles and target audience information

2. Include a time frame.

Is this your pre-launch strategy, launch, or post-launch? Combination of all?

3. Create a goals section.

Copy over your goals from the early chapters of your book. Your strategy should be designed to accomplish your main goal with the mini goals as your check-ins and milestones to achieving that.

Ex: If your book has already been published, you might have a strategy that is based on a big goal for the year, (ie, 10,000 books sold, or 100,000 email subscribers) with monthly goals broken down to meet the big goal. However you decide to do your strategy, it needs to have time goals included.

4. Establish your baseline immediately.

I suggest a spreadsheet or a chart in your marketing plan. Include your baseline numbers with the date of the data. I like to update this spreadsheet weekly so you can watch the growth.

\# of print books sold:

\# of ebooks sold:

Email list subscribers:

Followers on:

Facebook:

Instagram:

Twitter:

Pinterest:

Facebook group:

Views to the website for the week:

    For the month:

You may not be using all of those platforms, and that's okay. Just include what you are focusing on growing.

5. Include results from previous marketing attempts. If you have done previous advertising or marketing. If not, use your baseline to track any from here.

You might have run paid promos on Facebook or appeared on a Summit or podcast. What were the trackable results? Did your Amazon ads result in 100 book sales or just a cost of $x. Tracking your initial and ending "likes" or conversions at the beginning vs. the end, will show you over time how much ROI you are getting. Remember, in marketing for a newer author, sometimes ROI isn't clear and it builds and stacks over time.

6. Use your goals list to set up a time frame for what you are going to do and track the results using the tracker.

Start simple. And be realistic. Your goals can always be adjusted if necessary.

For example, if your goal is to grow your Instagram account by 1000 subscribers, you need to know that this takes time. So perhaps that is 1000 subscribers in 3 months. Break that down into weekly and daily goals. Then determine what you can do each day to work on that. (We actually have some bonus Instagram info for you in the chapter on Channels.)

7. List any focus areas or marketing "tools" you want to try to use in your strategy.

These may include: paid promo lists, a Virtual admin or part-time assistant to help with implementation, submission to awards programs, a focus on social media growth, email list growth, guest articles, podcast appearances. Then break each of these focus areas / tools down into tasks that need to happen for you to reach the goals, and in what time frame.

You can get REALLY detailed with these tasks... or you can give yourself enough of a checklist so that you know these are happening.

8. Determine your budget.

There are a variety of free things that you can do along the way, like engaging with people on Instagram, following hashtags on Twitter, etc. But there will be associated costs along the way. Hosting your website, buying your domain, etc. Take a look at the marketing activities you most want to do, determine the associated costs, and come up with a monthly budget.

*** Accounting tip. Keep track of every single expense and all receipts. Keep a spreadsheet where you can include the date, description, and cost. Almost everything you spend on your business can lower your tax liability.

9. Set a schedule and begin!

Congratulations. You now have the basis of how you're going to create your marketing strategy. Now it's a matter of using the tools to do the work.

10. Consider if you need a VA or other help.

It's a lot of work. You might find it is well worth your investment to pay someone for 3-5 hours a week to help you with some of these tasks so that you can spend more time writing your books!

Tool suggestion:

Use the goals sheets in this book to keep track of your weekly activities.

Trello is a great place for keeping checklists and to-dos, because you can just keep duplicating them for each time you repeat a marketing activity

QUICK NOTE: It's going to take hard, consistent work. But you will get there. It's a marathon, not a sprint.

The first part of your strategy is going to be all the key details and information about your actual book. It is really useful to keep all of the key data (metadata, etc) in one place anyway, because as you apply for different featured promos, book awards, review opportunities, and more, they will often ask for all of this info. It will save you a lot of time if you keep all of it in one easy to access file/location.

Sample Marketing Strategy:

Include all of the key areas from above. It may look something like this:

Key Book Data

Book Information:

Title:

Subtitle

Author Name (as it appears on the cover):

ISBNs:

Imprint:

Price:

Author Bio:

Brief Synopsis:

BISAC codes / primary category:

Other categories:

Key Marketing Data

Key Marketing Points: (the key marketing points are the Unique Selling Proposition—USP—or what makes your book different from others. It can also be the, "for readers who love books like x,y,z" (fiction) or it can be the key takeaways/key learning points in the book (nonfiction).

-

-

-

Keywords:

Hashtags:

Description of my target reader/target audience:

Groups/forums/places to engage with my target audience:

Endorsements: (or list people you would like to ask for endorsements)

Current Marketing Goals:

Current Marketing activities:

What is working:

What is not currently working or results not clear:

New tactics to try:

My Marketing Profile:

Things I Can Do:

Things I Would Like to Do:

Things I Enjoy Doing:

Things That Terrify Me:

Things that I'm interested in learning how to do:

Things I want to find someone else to do for me.

* * * *

Congratulations! If you've done all of that, you should have the beginning of a pretty robust marketing strategy!

Here are some common marketing activities:

- Guest blogging
- Blogging on Own Site
- Article submission
- Podcast interviews

- Launch your own podcast
- Summit Appearance
- Run Facebook Group
- Live video/ Facebook/IG Stories/YouTube etc.
- Listing your book on paid promo lists
- Library Events
- TV / Media appearances
- Influencer marketing
- Teaching course
- Book sales funnels
- Facebook Ads
- Pinterest
- Instagram
- BookBub
- Amazon Ads
- Blog Tours / Influencer Tours
- Advanced Review Team growth
- Netgalley & other early review sites
- Book Reviewers / Paid reviews
- Awards programs
- Newsletter Swaps

Things you should NOT do:

1. Do NOT Try to learn how to do every possible book marketing activity on your own. If you are on a limited budget, learn what you can and implement the low cost/free initiatives. If money isn't as tight, HIRE PEOPLE TO HELP!

2. Do NOT Try to become an expert in all things social media and marketing. Don't do it. Instead, focus on one place and become the expert there. (Make sure you start where you are most comfortable and where your target audience is actually present.) If you think Instagram would be a great place to grow your following and gain supporters/reviewers/true fans, perhaps consider hiring an instagram expert to get you started and a strategy in place for you. Many of them can do the research for you that may take hours, get you set up, and teach you how to keep it afloat. HIRE PEOPLE TO HELP!

3. Do NOT Try to implement an "everything" strategy. Pick a few tactics and spend some time getting really good at it.

I recently watched a woman grow her following from a couple thousand fans on Facebook to over ONE MILLION. In several months. She had one of the biggest book launches of an indie, first-time author I've ever seen. She did it by going live multiple times a day on Facebook and just sharing her funny day-to-day experiences. She showed up consistently and when she saw something that was working for her audience and getting a lot of engagement, she engaged back and created more content like that. Now she has brands knocking on her door, she's being invited to speaking events, etc.

She didn't try to conquer it all. She got on her cell phone and started posting some funny videos. And she shared them smartly. People loved it.

That doesn't have to be your thing. But you can find a "thing" and focus on doing more of that.

* * * *

I suggest you start a Google drive folder, or if you don't use Google Drive, a folder on your computer, backed up to an external drive or a cloud filing (preferably both).

Tips on file organization:

I create a folder system for each book. You can do this wherever you store your files, but always keep a backup someplace. We have the main folder (usually named by the book title.) Inside the folder I have:

- Final Files (I keep the very latest PDF and cover files)

- Interior files

- Cover files

- Ebook files

- Key documents & data

- Marketing strategy & assets

This type of filing helps me quickly locate all key information and resources when I'm publishing and promoting the book.

First document to create. Open a word doc or google doc and create your basic Book Marketing Data - key book info. Here is a sample of the type of information you should include in your document. Some of this you may not have available yet, but you can come back and fill it in later.

We include full sample strategies and templates in the Market Your Book! Course.

Weekly goals _____

Set aside at least 20 minutes at the start of each week to plan for the week. Specifically, when will you be working on marketing & what do you want to achieve?

My goal for the week is:

_____

_____

_____

Is there anything I need to do before I can work on this goal?

_____

_____

_____

On a scale of 1-10, how committed am I to achieving this one goal this week? 1 2 3 4 5 6 7 8 9 10

My baseline: (keep track of where you started this week. This will be based on your goals. So if it's social media growth, how many followers do you have today? If it's book sales or reviews, what is your starting number?)

_____

_____

_____

Don't Assume You Know Your Readers

amy collins

MARKETING EXPERT, FOREIGN RIGHTS AGENT

Amy Collins is the founder of Bestseller Builders and New Shelves Books. Collins is a trusted expert, speaker, and recommended sales consultant for some of the largest book and library retailers and wholesalers in the publishing industry. She is a USA TODAY and WALL STREET JOURNAL bestselling author and in the last 20 years, Amy and her team have sold over 40 Million books into the bookstore, library, and chain store market for small and midsized publishers. She is a columnist for and a board member of several publishing organizations. She has recently decided to take her experience as a bookseller and become an agent for authors, focusing on foreign rights.

It does not matter how you feel. Do "it" anyway. Actions come before feelings, not the other way around.

https://www.facebook.com/NewShelvesBooks
https://twitter.com/askamycollins

Genre: Nonfiction

It took me five years to stop ASSUMING I KNEW my readers and actually DO the research. When I was younger, I was guilty of believing everything I thought. I did not believe I had to research the market, i would just be able to use my own experiences to understand my target audience. NOPE! So glad I got over that.

TAKE THE TIME TO RESEARCH

Amy Collins has been successfully selling and marketing books for a long time, but has only started writing and publishing her own books in the last few years. She had the benefit of understanding what booksellers want to see in a book, but had to spend some time learning about the readers.

In order to further her knowledge on what is trending and selling well and better position her books and the books she is marketing, Amy pores over the bestseller lists every few days. And NOT just on Amazon! She recommends looking at Indie lists, USA TODAY, and also keep a watch on publishers marketplace. Amy recommends subscribing to Shelf-Awareness to see what big books are releasing, how they are being received, and how THEY are positioned.

Amy's best marketing tip for authors: "Other authors are not your competition, they are your community. GET OUT THERE and join in the conversation with your community." She is a firm believer that your best resource in learning how to be a more successful book marketer is by following and learning from other successful authors and publishers within your genre. You can use what they are doing and sharing to become a more educated, knowledgeable author and promoter. Bloggers, reviewers, tools, ads, contests.... you can learn a lot about what readers want by watching what the successful authors doing. Where are they hanging out? How are they marketing their books and connecting with their readers.

Amy has lots of tips and advice for authors on her website: http://www.newshelves.com/.

CHAPTER 6

growing your author platform

You now have the basics for starting your marketing strategy. As a first-time or relatively unknown author, a major focus of that strategy should be focused on growing your author platform.

WHAT IS AN AUTHOR PLATFORM AND WHY IS IT SO IMPORTANT?

"Author platform" is a term you'll hear frequently as an indie author. But what is it? Your author platform is your scope of influence as a writer. Simply put, it's your fans. The platform includes current readers and anyone who may become a reader in the future.

These are the people you hope to convert to "true fans." We talked about this concept earlier in the book, and I promised I'd return to the story about E.L. James, the author of 50 Shades of Grey. Touted by many as an "overnight success," it was actually her massive platform which played the most significant role in the book going "viral." How did an author, who originally self-published her book on Amazon, wind up selling over 150 million copies, only then to have her book become the #1 bestselling book in the history of Random House? I assure you, it was not because she wrote a steamy book, because many authors have done that before. It was her tireless effort at getting her writing in front of people long before the big publisher picked it up.

A lot of things came together to make that happen, but we

can start with one very basic attribution: when the book was published with Vintage Press, she already had a massive author platform and a whole lot of "buzz." Her already existing fan base of over five million people, that she grew from publishing her writing through Fanfiction.net, is largely responsible for the book's insane success. So write "buzzworthy" books! "Buzz" will sell your books. It's the number 1 thing, as a matter of fact.

Write content that people want to talk about and share. Word-of-mouth marketing will be your biggest tool to building a fanbase. "Buzz" is truly the factor that led to the enormous success of 50 Shades. This buzz was created by E.L. James' true fans. Upon re-publication with Vintage Press, the book debuted at the #1 spot on the NY Times combined print and eBook fiction bestseller list and stayed there for a very long time.

Many fiction authors will begin their writing on what's called "fanfic" sites, or something like Wattpad. It's a place you can just write and people see your work in progress. They can provide feedback and often become invested in your stories. E.L. James was writing and sharing and spending the time growing her fans, doing the work to build her author platform, without any idea of what that would mean in the future.

It was the fact that so many people were already talking about this self-published book that led Anne Messitte, publisher of Vintage Books, an imprint at Random House, to read a copy of it. In 2012, she received a copy that was being passed around her circles. She recognized that if a book was generating this much discussion, it would sell well. One thing led to another, and Vintage Books acquired the book. Messitte took a chance on this book, not because of sales data or because it fell within the types of books she normally published, but because of all of the activity around this book she saw online and in communities.

The five million fans that E.L. James had established through her fanfic audience played a tremendous role by buying the book when it was launched, reviewing it on Goodreads, and voting for it when she was in the running for the Goodreads Best Romance Book of the Year. They showed up as true fans and promoted the book on her behalf.

While not every author will have the same type of result as E.L. James did, every author can work to build their platform of true fans and reach a far greater level of success than without them. Your goal of building your platform is to get your fans to behave like this as well.

You can't create buzz without an audience. Full stop.

For fiction writers, the best way to build the platform is to just start writing fiction and getting it out there into the hands of readers. Yes, I am encouraging you to share your incomplete work, to give away your writing, and to grow your fans by getting them hooked on your storylines and characters.

For nonfiction, give value, create solutions to problems, spread your message far and wide.

FINDING READERS

This part is hard, even for seasoned writers, if you don't take the time to position yourself well where your readers will find you. These are places to find and cultivate relationships and learn about what the readers of your genre want. They are not places to rabidly promote your book.

These places include:

- Book clubs

- Networking, events

- Forums, like Goodreads (important - Goodreads is especially meant to be used to find and connect with readers AS A READER ... NOT to spam people about your book or promote.)

- Facebook groups

- Email promo lists

How do you know how to find those places? Research! Ask your existing readers. Talk to other authors. And get your book in front of known reviewers. This is going to serve you greatly in the early stages of building your author platform.

We'll dig into how you find these readers and reviewers next.

Key concepts to consider when growing your audience:

While building an email list is hands down one of the smartest things you can do, and building a following on social media, these are things that you can do over time and work on consistently.

In order to build that audience effectively, you've done the work to identify the target reader, and as you progress you need to focus on content creation. This might be more books, blog posts, social media content, growing a following on a site like BookBub, and so on. You'll want to start that process very early and do a LOT of it. Content marketing is still a very valuable tool for finding people, whether it's through blogging, or youtubing, or writing articles, or getting on podcasts.

Include time for researching these outlets into your strategy.

Finding Reviewers start early!

REVIEWS ARE YOUR GOLDEN TICKET

Here is the thing about reviews. There is almost nothing more important to a new/relatively unknown author than reviews. As an unknown author, people need to feel confident that buying your book is a good idea for them. Good reviews show them the things that are great about your book. And bad reviews help other people that would have the same issues NOT buy your book. By the way, bad reviews offer a lot of opportunities for us to fix things in future books, perhaps improve our sales copy, and let us know what our book is missing for people. So use them as an opportunity for improvement, not a reason to slide into depression.

The best way to get reviews is to seek out people that LOVE reading books and writing reviews. Sorry, friends, family, and colleagues are going to let you down in this department. It's just the truth.

Make sure your book marketing strategy focuses HEAVILY on getting reviews.

The following is a special essay by Nancy Cavillones, my right hand woman. She is the person on our team who is most focused on finding reviewers and coordinating our influencer campaigns before we launch a book. You can find all of her contact information in the case study following this chapter.

How To Find Book Reviewers
Nancy Cavillones

Word of mouth is the number one driver of book sales but word of mouth doesn't mean asking friends and family to spread the word about your book. Authors need to expand their reach by seeking out book bloggers and book influencers.

Your search for book reviewers should begin at least 5 months before your publication date. Why? You'll need time to do the research, craft your pitch and take advantage of book reviewers' turn-around times. Many book reviewers need 1-3 months lead time. If you want book reviews to coincide with your publication date, plan ahead!

Do The Research

Book bloggers and book influencers with significant reach are highly sought after, which allows them to be selective. You need to do your research. You are looking for book reviewers that are interested in your genre.

I start my research at BookSirens.com, using their book reviewer directory to scan for book bloggers that accept pitches in the genre of book I'm promoting.

Search results can be filtered according to who is currently accepting pitches, whether reviews are paid or free, and other criteria. Narrow down your results if necessary.

Each reviewer profile will give you a link to that reviewer's blog or other platform where reviews are published. Click through to each one you're interested in and look for submission guidelines. You'll want to follow these guidelines to the letter.

Use my tracking spreadsheet to get started, which you can grab from https://www.va4indieauthors.com/ reviewer-tracker. This spreadsheet will help you keep track of what you need to know about each book reviewer in order to send a personalized pitch.

Spend some time reading through the book reviewer's posts to get a feel for what kind of books they prefer. Your book may fall within their genre preference, but the reviewer may prefer a certain style of writing or have other tendencies.

Identify reviews they've written about books that are comparable to yours. You'll use this in your pitch to the reviewer.

Other places to find book reviewers

- https://www.feedspot.com/ is an RSS feed that allows you to search for specific types of blogs. When you search for book bloggers, you can even narrow it down by genre.
- Search #bookstagram on Instagram to generate a list of bookish Instagram accounts.
- Amazon: search for books in your genre and scroll down to the list of reviewers. Often, book bloggers will have profiles that contain contact information.

About Your Book

Real talk. Book reviewers expect professionally produced books. As a reviewer myself, I am drawn to well-designed covers. That gets me in the door. The book description needs to resonate with me. There is no point in investing time and money in finding book reviewers, or any marketing activity for that matter, if you don't invest in your BOOK. Understand the conventions of your genre, hire a book cover designer and craft a well-written book description.

WRITING THE PITCH

Once you've gathered information on the reviewers and made your list, the next step is writing the pitch.

Don't be lazy! Personalize your pitch. Book reviewers receive lots and lots of pitches, and can spot a template from a mile away. An effort to personalize your pitch will be appreciated.

Keep your pitch short and sweet. Do not include any attachments, unless it is specifically requested. I recommend that you create a page on your website for your media kit or one-sheet, so that you can direct reviewers to it, rather than attaching it to the email. Do not attach a copy of your book unless specifically requested in the reviewer guidelines.

You can use a service like BookFunnel, StoryOrigin or BookSirens to deliver a digital ARC, and include that link in the email.

This first contact is an invitation and an opportunity for the reviewer to decide if they want to work with you.

Your pitch to the book blogger should focus not on why your book is worth the read, but why you think the book blogger will be interested in it. If your book isn't worth the read, why are you asking anyone to read it? Instead, think about what it is about the book blogger that makes you think they'll enjoy your book.

Be respectful of turnaround times. If a book blogger says they will respond within a certain timeframe, do not follow up until that timeframe has passed without a response. If you send two emails without a response, let it go.

Be prepared to provide your book in the format requested by the book blogger. Some will take any format; many prefer .epub or .mobi files. If a book blogger requests a print copy, you'll have to decide whether it's worth the expense for you.

If a book reviewer charges a fee, they should have a media kit available that outlines their social media reach, their newsletter open rate, and other metrics that will help you determine whether the fee is a good value. If they do not have a media kit available, you'll have to find them on social media to see how many followers they have on the various social media platforms.

PATIENCE AND PERSISTENCE ARE THE KEY

Ultimately, getting book reviews is about building relationships. Make an effort to engage with book reviewers on their platforms. A few years ago, it was very easy to get a response from a book reviewer. These days, with the explosive growth in self-publishing, book reviewers are in high demand. You'll need to make yourself stand out, and the surest way to do that is show up, be present and engage. If you don't get a response from a book reviewer, don't take it personally. Many of them do this as a side gig and are not able to respond to each and every request. Following the guidelines outlined here will increase but not guarantee success. Keep going!

Thank you so much Nancy, for this great insight!

Now, as you set your weekly goals, I encourage you to focus on finding reviewers!

Be sure to check out our extra resources on the website!

Weekly goals _____

Set aside at least 20 minutes at the start of each week to plan for the week. Specifically, when will you be working on marketing & what do you want to achieve?

My goal for the week is:

_____

_____

_____

Is there anything I need to do before I can work on this goal?

_____

_____

_____

On a scale of 1-10, how committed am I to achieving this one goal this week? 1 2 3 4 5 6 7 8 9 10

My baseline: (keep track of where you started this week. This will be based on your goals. So if it's social media growth, how many followers do you have today? If it's book sales or reviews, what is your starting number?)

_____

_____

_____

ADVANCED READERS & REVIEWERS

nancy cavillones
VA & BOOK MARKETING ASSISTANT

Nancy Cavillones is an indie author's best friend and is on a mission to keep authors sane by handling the minutiae of their online presence and communications. She's been online in some form or other since 1993, and still has the AOL dial-up tone stuck in her head. She enjoys taking the scenic route, forcing her kids to appreciate nature, and spending time in New York City by herself in a desperate attempt to recapture her college days. Originally from Upstate NY by way of Long Island, Nancy currently lives in Los Gatos, CA with her husband, three children and one fat orange tabby named King. Nancy is the co-editor of Lose the Cape Mom's Guide to Becoming Socially and Politically Engaged (And Rising Tiny Activists, Too!).

Se Hace Camino Al Andar / You Make The Way By Walking

https://www.facebook.com/va4indieauthors
https://twitter.com/va4indieauthors

Genre: Nonfiction

Starting your marketing early and intentionally! Seek out reviewers to help you create a buzz around your book and put it in front of your target audience.

Let People With Experience Help You

Nancy became a virtual assistant in 2016 to create a more flexible work-life schedule. She says, "I got my start in author support as a member of the Write Publish Sell team, headed up by founder Alexa Bigwarfe, with whom I still work to this day. I discovered that working with authors was fulfilling and meaningful creative work, and I pivoted to signing on solely with indie authors in 2019. My strengths are helping authors navigate tech solutions for platform growth, and acting as a sounding board for marketing strategies."

Marketing your own book requires making it a priority over other activities and work and really requires a large investment of time and a focus on building relationships. Sometimes your best use of your budget is to allow someone else to do a lot of the legwork, like researching reviewers and influencers who might want to share about your book. There are lots of people who are experts at this and will do it for you efficiently. At the end of the process, you'll have a network and a list of contacts, without having to spend all the time to do the research on your own. No matter which route you take, be authentic and be people-forward.

Nancy's full interview can be found at https://writepublishsell. com/just-market-it-featured/.

To learn more about Nancy and her services to support authors, please visit http://va4indieauthors.com.

CHAPTER 7

marketing channels

The "channels" are the different places in which you carry forth your strategy. You can identify these as anything you want. Your "marketing channels" might be your blog, your social media accounts, or any fun tools you use, like Bublish.

When considering the multitude of channels, which I'll describe in further detail later in this channel, you may start to feel panicky. Because it can be a LOT, especially when looked at all clumped together. I want to make sure you know and understand that there are people and services to help you do these things, and not all of them cost a ridiculous amount of money. In fact, the amount of time and brain power you can save by investing $200 in someone else may be worth so much more in the long run.

The key thing about working with a marketing specialist, a publishing partner, or an assistant trained in supporting authors is that they are able to save you a ton of time and money by not only introducing you to channels of which you might not have been aware, but also will teach you the most effective way to use that channel. When you're considering all the many different facets of what you might need to be doing to market your book, any places you can take a shortcut to a faster reward on your efforts is a bonus. Throughout this book we have introduced you to many people and services that you might want to consider. You'll also find more information on our special resources.

When it comes to the vast amount of knowledge you need to be a successful author, some people do not want to take on the burden of learning every single detail. Which is why partner publishers/hybrid publishing/self-publishing assist companies have grown so rapidly.

One of my authors, a very special author, Kasie Whitener (After

December, published by Chrysalis Press, 2019) told me that she found that one of the greatest pieces of value of working with me as a publisher was that I laid out the channels for her that she needed in order to position herself and build her platform.

No matter what route to publishing you take, unless you are picked up by a huge publisher, marketing and building your fan base is always a primary responsibility of the author.

Sometimes it takes someone with a little more experience in the publishing industry to make you realize the importance of doing things you didn't think were important before you had a book to sell.

Kasie shared, "I had never really thought about the need for an email list because I didn't think I had a message to share yet. Since I hadn't completed my book and didn't really have anything to market, I didn't understand the importance of getting in front of my Generation X audience. After the launch, I realized that there was so much more I could have done far in advance."

Her book is a story of friendship and forgiveness, set in the late 90s. While her main category / genre is definitely literary fiction and women's fiction - "literary fiction" is not an audience. When determining "Who is this book for?" it's definitely for Generation X women who remember being in their late teens / early twenties in the 90s. They loved movies like Reality Bites and have read books like Ethan Hawke's The Hottest State. They can sing the lyrics to the Counting Crows "Long December" and remember that era with much nostalgia.

The experience of launching her book and realizing, oh, snap, I could have done so much more!, was eye opening for Kasie, but it also taught her so much and she's made major changes in her content marketing strategy as she continues to build her audience in anticipation of her second book.

Use as Many Channels As You Can

kasie whitener

FICTION AUTHOR & BUSINESS CONSULTANT

Dr. Kasie Whitener writes GenX fiction and blogs for the South Carolina Libertarian Party. Her debut novel, After December, has been called "a breakthrough debut" and "outstanding fiction." Her day job is business owner at Clemson Road Creative and lecturer at the Darla Moore School of Business at the University of South Carolina. At her core is fantasy romance and not-quite-getting-over-the-90s. She hosts two weekly writer events on Twitter (#wschat) and local radio (@WriteOnSC). Dr. Whitener has presented workshops for the South Carolina Council on Humanities, Bowling Green State University's Winter Wheat Literary Festival, the Pat Conroy Literary Center, and Fairfax County Public Library.

"Never let the fear of striking out keep you from playing the game." Babe Ruth

https://www.facebook.com/kasiewhitener
https://twitter.com/KasieWhitener

Genre: Fiction (Literary)

Content is king. The more you can show what you know, teach others usable skills, or add to the discussion, the more you are contributing to the industry, not just selling something. Use as many marketing channels as you can to share your content. Start building your email list early, because even if your book hasn't published yet, you still have something to say.

PLAY THE LONG GAME WITH AUDIENCE GROWTH

Kasie and I have talked a lot about her marketing, the channels she is using, and what she wants to see as she prepares to begin marketing for her second book.

Kasie said, "Despite establishing a great network and a strong social media presence, I didn't have a product—a book! —to market. So when it came time to tell people about the book, I was behind the curve. I didn't have an email subscribers list. I struggled for a while finding my voice (since I have multiple blogs) and deciding how much of myself I wanted to reveal in my marketing efforts. I also needed branding which should have evolved out of my voice but I couldn't really decide who I wanted to present to the world."

Something happened to Kasie when she turned 40. She described it as feeling like all bets were off. "Be Yourself" became her new motto and it became crystal clear that she, like her target reader, identify as "UnapologeticallyX." As she connected more with that brand, it opened something for her, giving her more courage to write about politics on her website and wrap her brand around my characters' experience of coming-of-age in the 90s. A lot of writers hide behind their work but she wanted to burst forth through hers.

"It's challenging, it's gritty, and it's X. And so am I."

When it comes to building her target audience and reader platform, Kasie shared:

"As an author, you have to accept that some people won't like that. Which is fine. I've struggled with really finding my target market—my ideal reader—and being comfortable with the fact that it won't be everyone. Some people (old men, looking at you) won't get me. And that's got to be okay. To be authentic, I have to be brave enough to let the haters go."

Her best advice is for you to become a more educated, knowledgeable author and promoter. Bloggers, reviewers, tools, ads, contests.... you can learn a lot about what readers want by watching what the successful authors doing.

Learn more about Kasie and her books at http://afterdecember.com.

marketing channels

Here are some of the common "channels" for marketing your book:

- Social media
- Paid advertising - Facebook ads, Amazon Ads, Google Ads, traditional ads
- Promo sites and lists - Bookbub, Fussy Librarian
- Review sites - Netgalley
- Editorial reviews
- Influencer marketing / summits / podcasts / guest blogging
- Blogging / content marketing
- Conferences and events
- Libraries
- Larger distribution - Ingram, Kobo, PublishDrive
- Marketing tools / apps - Bublish, Bookfunnel
- Book sales funnels
- Publicity, PR reps, media appearances

And we could list many more.

It's no wonder most authors feel overwhelmed! It's a full-time job just to keep up with managing all of these elements. You don't have to try all of these and you certainly shouldn't attempt to start all at the same time.

It's not always easy to determine which are the best for you and what will be the best way for you to spend your time and energies as you explore them. This is a major focus in my course, Growing Your Author Platform: https://writepublishsell.thinkific.com/courses/author-platform.

Is Advertising Required to Sell Books?

I believe so. In some form. Advertising is not a nice-to-have for authors anymore who want to see big sales. It's a requirement. I don't talk a lot about advertising because that is a more advanced marketing tactic, but we certainly get into it through our more in depth marketing programs and consulting.

What about publicists, TV spots,and high profile interviews? Is this a requirement?

I'm so glad you asked this question because I have some REAL data to share on this.

Last year, we published an incredible book that is a resource the world needs. *What do I Do? A Step by Step Guide for Friends and Family to Support Anyone Who Has Lost a Child* by Kimberly Calabrese. Kim, whose infant daughter died unexpectedly, has spent years connecting with grieving parents and interviewing them about what they needed in the days, weeks, and months after their child died. She knew that this is a resource that those closest to the family needed to have so that they could support their friend or family member after such a tragic loss.

It is a necessary book, but unfortunately, not the type of book that people buy "just in case." Kim had an incredible publicist that had her booked on major TV shows and stations, plus radio shows and podcasts all over the United States. Kim did a fabulous job spreading her message and informing people about the book.

But very few people bought the book. Because they didn't need it at that time. We were completely dumbfounded by the lack of sales after this massive PR campaign. We quickly realized that is a fabulous campaign for someone who has a summer blockbuster, or an audience that is eager to buy right away. Her audience will only buy this book when it is necessary.

So we re-thought the strategy. Who WOULD be buying a book

like this? Well, school guidance counselors, bereavement experts, funeral homes, hospitals, perhaps clergy members, counselors, school principals, HR managers. The book covers helping a bereaved parent return to work, supporting the siblings as they return to school, and so forth.

Future marketing endeavors will focus on those groups. Conferences and workshops for HR managers, funeral home directors, CEOs, teachers, principals, counselors. They are the audience that sees the value in not only knowing that information ahead of time, but having it in their libraries to give to the people that they work with on a daily basis that need this information.

So a channel for you might be professional conferences in your niche. When you think about your marketing strategies and where you want to show up, you also have to think about the audience of those programs. Generally speaking, the people watching morning news shows are stay at home moms and retirees. So if you've got a book that is relevant to that audience, or if you have a book that is one that people will want to rush right out to order once they see an interview with you, by all means, schedule the publicity campaign.

Was it a total waste of time and money? My experience tells me not even a little bit! We don't know what Kim's media appearances will eventually lead to. Publicity and media is out there forever. Who knows when someone will stumble across a podcast interview or media appearance and reach out to Kim?

That is another piece of the Long Game puzzle. You may not see immediate results of a marketing campaign. But that doesn't mean it isn't building toward something.

So recognize that ROI can't always be captured. But rest assured, if you are putting content out into the world and people are seeing it, you are building something. You are building name recognition.

WHERE SHOULD I START?

The best places for new authors to start is generally with a basic website to begin capturing email addresses and through the social media channel you think resonates most with your target audience!

We utilize Facebook and Instagram as our primary channels for audience building. We know that many of our target readers for the books we are publishing love Instagram. Instagram also allows for video and highlights and all kind of fun things.

I rely 100% on my team for implementing our Instagram Strategy. So I'm going to let you hear from Raewyn Sangari, the genius behind every Instagram book launch we do for my books and for any of the authors we publish.

Weekly goals _____

Set aside at least 20 minutes at the start of each week to plan for the week. Specifically, when will you be working on marketing & what do you want to achieve?

My goal for the week is:

_____

_____

_____

Is there anything I need to do before I can work on this goal?

_____

_____

_____

On a scale of 1-10, how committed am I to achieving this one goal this week? 1 2 3 4 5 6 7 8 9 10

My baseline: (keep track of where you started this week. This will be based on your goals. So if it's social media growth, how many followers do you have today? If it's book sales or reviews, what is your starting number?)

_____

_____

_____

The Power of Instagram for Authors

raewyn sangari
UNICORN VA & INSTAGRAM EXPERT

With soul talks, girl dates and coffee fueling her soul, Raewyn is a unicorn virtual assistant for high-vibe heart-centered female entrepreneurs. Instagram became Raewyn's happy place - finding community after the birth of her daughter. Through years as a blogger with a Journalism degree, Raewyn's Instagram obsession became an advantage for her clients. Pairing up with Alexa Bigwarfe of Write|Publish|Sell, Raewyn began working with authors to market their books. She has helped fiction, non-fiction, and children's authors to have successful bestselling launches. Raewyn is a mama bear to a strong-willed daughter and easygoing son, and wife to her high school best friend. She truly believes that every woman is a strong woman capable of self-love, self-confidence and achieving the goals in the deepest corners of her heart.

Develop enough courage so that you can stand up for yourself and then stand up for somebody else. - Maya Angelou

www.facebook.com/raewynsangari
https://instagram.com/unicornvabasics

It's all about CONNECTING with your readers.

You don't have to post on Instagram every single day, but you need to be connecting with your followers.

You don't have to consistently post on Instagram to use it as a marketing tool. Forgetting about Instagram leaves valuable real estate open!

INSTAGRAM FOR AUTHORS

Instagram is an underutilized social media marketing platform because of the intricacies of it. Is it just a place to share photographs and videos? Do you have to have amazing high-quality photos to gain a large following?

Nope! Also, you probably don't want a massive following either because it makes your engagement lower. Understanding the Instagram algorithm isn't as difficult as understanding Facebook's business page algorithm, but it can still be challenging for someone who is trying to launch a book. That's where I come in!

Having worked with several authors on their Instagram strategy, book launch and engagement, I have worked out a unique marketing technique. While the overall strategy might mirror other platforms, like using influencers, I help you to build actual connection with your readers.

For an author, I offer an Instagram strategy, regular Instagram posting, a book launch special, and a new "Instagram Book Page" package.

I offer several levels of Instagram strategy and management. My most popular package is a book launch special. With a special strategy focused on launching your book successfully, I take

Instagram off of your plate during your busiest time! Launch week festivities are crucial, and I'll make sure your Instagram is doing the part it needs to play in getting eyes on your book.

Learn more about Raewyn's services for authors here: http://www.raewynsangari.com/justmarketit

CHAPTER 8

the long game

Whew! It certainly has felt like a long journey to get us to this point. And we're just getting started. You'll hear all the sports cliches when it comes to marketing your book. I use them too. Because there is no better analogy. It's the long game. We've got to play all four quarters. It's a marathon, not a sprint. You can't just push hard to your launch day (let's say the end of the 1st quarter) and then leave the field. Or you will lose.

Just like you'd want to train and work from a plan with running a marathon or playing on a winning team, to be successful with your as an author, you also have to have a plan and be invested in the plan until you're no longer interested in selling books.

The truth is, marketing is the hardest thing you'll ever do for your books. So if you thought writing and revising was difficult ... you're in for a shock.

BUT... there is good news! Despite the fact that I just loaded you down with a ton of work and research to do, marketing can also be a lot of fun. The best part is, it allows you to develop relationships with your readers, with other experts in your industry, and other authors.

The interesting thing about marketing is that there are so many different ways to approach it, and there is no right or wrong answer. There are goals and objectives and certainly tried and true methods, but since you as the author are the primary tool for marketing, everything you do has to feel authentic and good for you. This allows for a lot of creativity and flexibility, but it does not allow for taking the easy way out.

I have a broad range of experience in marketing, digital marketing, sales, and most importantly, book launches and marketing. I think that my varied background has really helped me understand the mindset around sales, the fear of putting yourself out there to sell something, and the buyer mindset. But what I've loved the most about it all is that at the heart of marketing is relationship building. When you approach marketing from the perspective of a service to others and providing value, authentically, it does not seem as difficult.

I've provided a lot of information in this book. You may find that you've got a lot of other learning to do before you can tackle some of the more advanced marketing options. Do that later. First... you now have the basic foundations for establishing your marketing efforts. You don't have to do everything in this book and you don't have to do it all in 90 days. But you do have to start somewhere and take consistent, goal-based action steps.

Use the weekly goals sheet found at the end of each chapter and use that as a basis to map out the next 90 days of your marketing strategy.

Do the work to find your target audience and create your marketing strategy.

Then implement.

When the first 90 days are over, set goals for the following 90 days and do this again.

Those who want to win the game as an author will work at this until they don't have to anymore.

You've got this!

Don't forget the extra resources for you to use at https://writepublishsell.com/JMI-secret. Password: JMIrocks

Weekly goals _____

Set aside at least 20 minutes at the start of each week to plan for the week. Specifically, when will you be working on marketing & what do you want to achieve?

My goal for the week is:

_____

_____

_____

Is there anything I need to do before I can work on this goal?

_____

_____

_____

On a scale of 1-10, how committed am I to achieving this one goal this week? 1 2 3 4 5 6 7 8 9 10

My baseline: (keep track of where you started this week. This will be based on your goals. So if it's social media growth, how many followers do you have today? If it's book sales or reviews, what is your starting number?)

_____

_____

_____

START MARKETING EARLY & CONSISTENTLY!

Angela J. Ford

FANTASY AUTHOR & MARKETING STRATEGIST

Angela J. Ford is a bestselling epic fantasy author who has sold almost 30,000 copies and has had over 10 million page reads in Kindle Unlimited. Her books have been ranked bestsellers in multiple categories. First and foremost, Angela is a reader and can often be found with her nose in a book. Aside from writing she enjoys the challenge of working with marketing technology and builds websites for authors.

Angela is passionate about helping indie authors succeed and runs a community and podcast called Indie Author Lifestyle. She enjoys traveling, hiking, and playing World of Warcraft with her husband.

"If you want to go fast, go alone. If you want to go far, go together."
African Proverb

https://www.facebook.com/angelajfordauthor
https://twitter.com/aford21

Genre: Fiction (Fantasy)

Start. Now. Often times we wait for everything to be perfect before we get started but you'll learn so much when you begin, so start now.

START EARLY; GROW YOUR EMAIL LIST

Angela published her first book, an epic fantasy novel, *The Five Warriors*. She had the advantage of having worked in marketing for three years with nonfiction authors and really developed an understanding for good marketing strategy and how to launch books. She also learned that marketing fiction books and understanding the target audience of fiction books is a lot easier than the nonfiction world, from her experience.

However, while she found the marketing tactics easier, she struggled with getting in front of that audience and getting enough reviews. Which is why she because such a fan of starting as early as possible with consistent activities to grow that reader base.

When it came to identifying her target audience, this was really easy for Angela, because she is her target audience. She reads the kinds of books she writes, and she already is in the discussion groups and forums with those readers. But it was still not easy to make her books visible to all of those readers. She learned that a big part of this was making sure she understood the genre well enough to make sure she had good cover designs that would be competitive, great sales page description, and all of her meta data was solid. This is just as important as the efforts to get the eyes on your book, because once you get traffic to the book page, you want them to actually buy the book!

Over the course of growing her fanbase, Angela partnered with other authors in her genre and did cross promotions, newsletter swaps, and relevant giveaways to entice people to read her book. These also helped her grow her email list significantly! *Angela also swears by the importance of a strong email list. A regular guest on the Women in Publishing Summit, (womeninpublishingsummit.com) Angela shared in her most recent interview about many more sales she sees when she sends out emails about her books. She tracks the sales in conjunction with a promo email about her books and notes that when she sends out a book specifically directing people to her book sales links, she always has a spike in sales.*

As mentioned previously, though, it doesn't happen overnight. Angela's marketing efforts were consistent and took time to result in profit. It also took the addition of more books to her series. It also takes financial investment. Angela shared: "It took me three years to break even on all my books. Once I finished my first epic fantasy series, I bundled them as a box set. I spent around $10,000 on expenses and marketing the box set and ended up with a profit of $50,000 for the year.

Angela publishes at least one book per year and continues to grow her list of titles, which is a large part of growing her revenue from books and her fanbase. She continues to employ consistent marketing efforts, and has branched out into other areas for sources of revenue, such as marketing for authors, building websites for authors, and running a community and podcast to support indie authors. The additional revenue from these sources allow her to focus on writing more books.

Her tips: Study the bestsellers in your genre and make your book competive. Start building your email list and showing up in front of your audience as early as you can. Talk to other authors, listen to their advice, and don't be afraid to take some risks.

Angela's interview from her first appearance with the Women in Publishing Summit can be found at https://writepublishsell.com/just-market-it-featured/.

To learn more about Angela, her books, and her services, please visit https://www.angelajford.com.

Planning
WEEKLY GOALS

This section is for those of you who need the space to write down goals and keep track of your accomplishments.

WEEK1_____

WEEK2_____

WEEK3_____

WEEK4_____

WEEK5_____

WEEK6_____

WEEK7_____

WEEK8_____

WEEK9_____

WEEK10_____

WEEK11_____

WEEK12_____

Did you ever consider your book could be something you do in gratitude to your readers / clients? If you put gratitude as your top priority, you'll go farther!

SHOWCASE YOUR EXPERTISE OFTEN!

Roshanda Pratt

STORY TELLING STRATEGIST

Roshanda 'The Rosho' Pratt is a digital media pioneer with 20 years experience as a news producer on the frontlines of history. She is a respected news producer, live stream expert, speaker, and storyteller strategist. With two decades of experience in crisis communications, marketing, and on both sides of the television camera. Her mission is to raise up messengers who willshape the narrative through media.Roshanda helps entrepreneurs and organizations amplify their message and transform communities. She is also a two time Amazon best-selling author, Huffington Post contributor, and host of her own self-produced Facebook Live show, "The Rosho Live." When she's not "going live", she is creating her greatest story with her husband and children in South Carolina.

"I got my start by giving myself a start!" Madam C. J. Walker

https://www.facebook.com/therosholive
https://twitter.com/therosholive

Genre: Nonfiction

The biggest struggle I think for many authors is using media to get more eyes on your book. How do you separate your book or standout from other authors? This can be overwhelming and frustrating if you do not have a plan.

SHOW UP EVERYWHERE!

Roshanda is passionate about encouraging authors and business owners to utilize live video! This is a great way to position yourself as an authority. When you write a (nonfiction) book, it is an extension of your expertise. You can use video/speaking opportunities to go beyond the surface of it is a good book. Educate your audience. People want value. Showcase the value or the why of the book. People buy the why.

Roshanda loves to teach. You can use Facebook, YouTube, Instagram stories, and other tools to make videos and educate your audience about ideas or concepts from the book.

Roshanda put this tip into practice and hosted her own virtual book signing. She taught from my book and had a paypal link so people could buy the book as she was teaching concepts from it.

She said, "I had another person monitoring it and and when someone purchased, I thanked them live on my video and signed their book on the spot. People loved it."

Roshanda also credits consistency to her success with her book - both in the message she delivered and in delivery over months of time.

Reduce the Overwhelm
BITE SIZE CHUNKS

We've talked about a lot of different pieces of what you need to know to build the foundation for marketing your book. You may feel super overwhelmed at this point. You may feel really nervous that you'll never be able to do all of these things. I assure you, you will. Now it's time to actually sit down and implement. If you plan some time each day to take action, you will find that it feels far less overwhelming.

You should really understand by this point that good marketing comes from a good plan and consistent action. You can have all the dreams in the world, but if you don't set out a plan to help you accomplish them, you are unlikely to see progress.

The following section of the book is a place for you to use to create your implementation schedule so that you will stick to doing the work. I like 90 days for the purpose of really solidifying this as a habit, but your marketing should go on and on and on for EVER. After 90 days of doing this, you may not need to keep a written weekly plan.

In the following "journal" section, you will find have a space to craft your goals for the week, followed by pages for daily goals.

Scope out your plan, schedule your marketing time, plug in what you will do each day to work toward accomplishing your goals, and get to work!

You've got this! Ditch the fear and just MARKET it!

90 Day Goal Tracker

Use this Weekly and Daily Goal Tracker to Set the Habit of Daily Action Steps to Create and Implement Your Marketing Strategy

Week 1: Day 1
SUNDAY, WEEK OF _ _/_ _/_ _

Set aside at least 20 minutes each Monday to set yourself up for the week ahead. Refer back to the weekly goals and fill them in your first weeks goal here. Specifically, when will you be marketing?

My goal for the week is:

_____

_____

_____

What do I need to do before I can move forward with this goal?

_____

_____

_____

On a scale of 1-10, how committed am I to achieving this one goal this week?

1 2 3 4 5 6 7 8 9 10

What am I most proud of for accomplishing so far?

_____

_____

_____

MONTH _____ / _____

I CAN TOTALLY SMASH THIS.

2

MY MARKETING FOCUS FOR TODAY IS:

_____

_____

TODAY'S 3 ACTION STEPS TO ACHIEVE MY WEEKLY GOAL:

_____

_____

_____

MONTH _____ / ____

I'M GONNA WIN OVER THIS.

3

MY MARKETING FOCUS FOR TODAY IS:

_____

_____

TODAY'S 3 ACTION STEPS TO ACHIEVE MY WEEKLY GOAL:

_____

_____

4

MONTH_____/_____
THIS IS WHAT I'M DOING.

MY MARKETING FOCUS FOR TODAY IS:

_____

_____

TODAY'S 3 ACTION STEPS TO ACHIEVE MY WEEKLY GOAL:

_____

_____

_____

5

MONTH_____/_____
IT'S OK TO CATCH UP IF I GET BEHIND.

MY MARKETING FOCUS FOR TODAY IS:

_____

_____

TODAY'S 3 ACTION STEPS TO ACHIEVE MY WEEKLY GOAL:

_____

_____

MONTH _____ / _____

WRAP THIS BABY UP.

6

MY MARKETING FOCUS FOR TODAY IS:

_____

_____

TODAY'S 3 ACTION STEPS TO ACHIEVE MY WEEKLY GOAL:

_____

_____

_____

MONTH _____ / _____

REFLECT & REWARD

7

MY MARKETING FOCUS FOR TODAY IS:

_____

_____

TODAY'S 3 ACTION STEPS TO ACHIEVE MY WEEKLY GOAL:

_____

_____

MARKETING IS YOUR JOB! DO IT!

Na'Ima B. Robert

AUTHOR & PUBLISHING COACH

Na'ima B. Robert is a trail-blazing speaker, coach and best-selling author of 'From My Sisters' Lips', as well as over 20 other books that have been translated into over 14 languages. She is the recipient of several literary awards and is a respected author of diverse fiction. She was the founder of SISTERS Magazine and Editor-in Chief for ten years, touching the lives of thousands of readers and launching the careers of dozens of writers. As a high level coach and author career strategist, she uses her training and experience to help women all over the world show up strong, tell their story and share their message with the world.

There are people out there who are waiting for you to step up. They need your message now.

https://www.facebook.com/ Naima-B-Robert-25192183771/
https://twitter.com/NaimaBRobert

Na'Ima shares: If I had to do it all over again, I would start building my MAILING LIST and creating products much sooner!

Week 2: Day 8

SUNDAY, WEEK OF __/__/__

Set aside at least 20 minutes each Monday to set yourself up for the week ahead. Refer back to the weekly goals and fill them in your first weeks goal here. Specifically, when will you be marketing?

My goal for the week is:

_____

_____

_____

What do I need to do before I can move forward with this goal?

_____

_____

_____

On a scale of 1-10, how committed am I to achieving this one goal this week?

1 2 3 4 5 6 7 8 9 10

What am I most proud of for accomplishing so far?

_____

_____

_____

9

I CAN TOTALLY SMASH THIS.

MY MARKETING FOCUS FOR TODAY IS:

_____

_____

TODAY'S 3 ACTION STEPS TO ACHIEVE MY WEEKLY GOAL:

_____

_____

_____

10

MONTH_____ / _____
I'M GONNA WIN OVER THIS.

MY MARKETING FOCUS FOR TODAY IS:

_____

_____

TODAY'S 3 ACTION STEPS TO ACHIEVE MY WEEKLY GOAL:

_____

_____

_____

MONTH _____/ ____
THIS IS WHAT I'M DOING.

11

MY MARKETING FOCU FOR TODAY IS:

_____

_____

TODAY'S 3 ACTION STEPS TO ACHIEVE MY WEEKLY GOAL:

_____

_____

_____

MONTH _____/ _____
IT'S OK TO CATCH UP IF I GET BEHIND.

12

MY MARKETING FOCUS FOR TODAY IS:

_____

_____

TODAY'S 3 ACTION STEPS TO ACHIEVE MY WEEKLY GOAL:

13

MONTH _____ / _____

WRAP THIS BABY UP.

MY MARKETING FOCUS FOR TODAY IS:

_____

_____

TODAY'S 3 ACTION STEPS TO ACHIEVE MY WEEKLY GOAL:

_____

_____

_____

14

MONTH_____ / _____

REFLECT & REWARD

MY MARKETING FOCUS FOR TODAY IS:

_____

TODAY'S 3 ACTION STEPS TO ACHIEVE MY WEEKLY GOAL:

Week 3: Day 15
SUNDAY, WEEK OF __ / __ / __

Set aside at least 20 minutes each Monday to set yourself up for the week ahead. Refer back to the weekly goals and fill them in your first weeks goal here. Specifically, when will you be marketing?

My goal for the week is:

_____

_____

_____

What do I need to do before I can move forward with this goal?

_____

_____

_____

On a scale of 1-10, how committed am I to achieving this one goal this week?

1 2 3 4 5 6 7 8 9 10

What am I most proud of for accomplishing so far?

_____

_____

_____

"DO SOMETHING EVERY DAY TO MARKET EACH OF YOUR BOOKS FOR THREE YEARS."
— JOHN KREMER

MONTH _____ / _____

I CAN TOTALLY SMASH THIS.

16

MY MARKETING FOCUS FOR TODAY IS:

_____

_____

TODAY'S 3 ACTION STEPS TO ACHIEVE MY WEEKLY GOAL:

_____

_____

_____

MONTH _____ / _____

I'M GONNA WIN OVER THIS.

17

MY MARKETING FOCUS FOR TODAY IS:

_____

_____

TODAY'S 3 ACTION STEPS TO ACHIEVE MY WEEKLY OOAL.

18

MONTH _____/_____

THIS IS WHAT I'M DOING.

MY MARKETING FOCUS FOR TODAY IS:

_____

_____

TODAY'S 3 ACTION STEPS TO ACHIEVE MY WEEKLY GOAL:

_____

_____

_____

19

MONTH _____/_____

IT'S OK TO CATCH UP IF I GET BEHIND.

MY MARKETING FOCUS FOR TODAY IS:

_____

_____

TODAY'S 3 ACTION STEPS TO ACHIEVE MY WEEKLY GOAL:

MONTH _____ / _____

20

MY MARKETING FOCUS FOR TODAY IS:

_____

_____

TODAY'S 3 ACTION STEPS TO ACHIEVE MY WEEKLY GOAL:

_____

_____

_____

MONTH _____ / _____

REFLECT & REWARD

21

MY MARKETING FOCUS FOR TODAY IS:

_____

_____

TODAY'S 3 ACTION STEPS TO ACHIEVE MY WEEKLY GOAL:

Week 4: Day 22
SUNDAY, WEEK OF __ / __ / __

Set aside at least 20 minutes each Monday to set yourself up for the week ahead. Refer back to the weekly goals and fill them in your first weeks goal here. Specifically, when will you be marketing?

My goal for the week is:

_____

_____

_____

What do I need to do before I can move forward with this goal?

_____

_____

_____

On a scale of 1-10, how committed am I to achieving this one goal this week?

1 2 3 4 5 6 7 8 9 10

What am I most proud of for accomplishing so far?

_____

_____

_____

MONTH _____ / _____

CAN TOTALLY SMASH THIS.

23

MY MARKETING FOCUS FOR TODAY IS:

_____

_____

TODAY'S 3 ACTION STEPS TO ACHIEVE MY WEEKLY GOAL:

_____

_____

_____

MONTH _____ / _____

I'M GONNA WIN OVER THIS.

24

MY MARKETING FOCUS FOR TODAY IS:

_____

_____

TODAY'S 3 ACTION STEPS TO ACHIEVE MY WEEKLY GOAL:

25

MONTH _____ / _____

THIS IS WHAT I'M DOING.

MY MARKETING FOCUS FOR TODAY IS:

_____

_____

TODAY'S 3 ACTION STEPS TO ACHIEVE MY WEEKLY GOAL:

_____

_____

_____

26

MONTH _____ / _____

IT'S OK TO CATCH UP IF I GET BEHIND.

MY MARKETING FOCUS FOR TODAY IS:

_____

_____

TODAY'S 3 ACTION STEPS TO ACHIEVE MY WEEKLY GOAL:

_____

_____

MONTH _____ / _____

WRAP THIS BABY UP.

27

MY MARKETING FOCUS FOR TODAY IS:

_____

_____

TODAY'S 3 ACTION STEPS TO ACHIEVE MY WEEKLY GOAL:

_____

_____

_____

MONTH _____ / _____

REFLECT & REWARD

28

MY MARKETING FOCUS FOR TODAY IS:

_____

_____

TODAY'S 3 ACTION STEPS TO ACHIEVE MY WEEKLY GOAL:

Week 5: Day 29
SUNDAY, WEEK OF __ / __ / __

Set aside at least 20 minutes each Monday to set yourself up for the week ahead. Refer back to the weekly goals and fill them in your first weeks goal here. Specifically, when will you be marketing?

My goal for the week is:

_____

_____

_____

What do I need to do before I can move forward with this goal?

_____

_____

_____

On a scale of 1-10, how committed am I to achieving this one goal this week?

1 2 3 4 5 6 7 8 9 10

What am I most proud of for accomplishing so far?

_____

_____

_____

MONTH _____ / _____

I CAN TOTALLY SMASH THIS.

20

MY MARKETING FOCUS FOR TODAY IS:

_____

_____

TODAY'S 3 ACTION STEPS TO ACHIEVE MY WEEKLY GOAL:

_____

_____

_____

MONTH _____ / _____

I'M GONNA WIN OVER THIS.

31

MY MARKETING FOCUS FOR TODAY IS:

_____

_____

TODAY'S 3 ACTION STEPS TO ACHIEVE MY WEEKLY GOAL:

_____

_____

32

MONTH _____/____

THIS IS WHAT I'M DOING.

MY MARKETING FOCUS FOR TODAY IS:

_____

_____

TODAY'S 3 ACTION STEPS TO ACHIEVE MY WEEKLY GOAL:

_____

_____

_____

33

MONTH _____/____

IT'S OK TO CATCH UP IF I GET BEHIND.

MY MARKETING FOCUS FOR TODAY IS:

_____

_____

TODAY'S 3 ACTION STEPS TO ACHIEVE MY WEEKLY GOAL:

_____

_____

_____

MONTH ___/ _____ **34**
WRAP THIS BABY UP.

MY MARKETING FOCUS FOR TODAY IS:

_____

_____

TODAY'S 3 ACTION STEPS TO ACHIEVE MY WEEKLY GOAL:

_____

_____

_____

MONTH _____/ _____ **35**
REFLECT & REWARD

HOW FAR DID I GET AT ACHIEVING MY GOAL?

_____

WHAT CAN I DO BETTER NEXT WEEK?

_____

I TOTALLY ROCKED IT! TO REWARD MYSELF I WILL. .

_____

_____

_____

Week 6: Day 36
SUNDAY, WEEK OF __ / __ / __

Set aside at least 20 minutes each Monday to set yourself up for the week ahead. Refer back to the weekly goals and fill them in your first weeks goal here. Specifically, when will you be marketing?

My goal for the week is:

_____

_____

_____

What do I need to do before I can move forward with this goal?

_____

_____

_____

On a scale of 1-10, how committed am I to achieving this one goal this week?

1 2 3 4 5 6 7 8 9 10

What am I most proud of for accomplishing so far?

_____

_____

_____

37

MONTH _____/_____
I CAN TOTALLY SMASH THIS.

MY MARKETING FOCUS FOR TODAY IS:

_____

_____

TODAY'S 3 ACTION STEPS TO ACHIEVE MY WEEKLY GOAL:

_____

_____

_____

38

MONTH _____/_____
I'M GONNA WIN OVER THIS.

MY MARKETING FOCUS FOR TODAY IS:

_____

_____

TODAY'S 3 ACTION STEPS TO ACHIEVE MY WEEKLY GOAL:

_____

_____

_____

39

MONTH _____/____
THIS IS WHAT I'M DOING.

MY MARKETING FOCUS FOR TODAY IS:

_____

_____

TODAY'S 3 ACTION STEPS TO ACHIEVE MY WEEKLY GOAL:

_____

_____

_____

40

MONTH _____/____
IT'S OK TO CATCH UP IF I GET BEHIND.

MY MARKETING FOCUS FOR TODAY IS:

_____

_____

TODAY'S 3 ACTION STEPS TO ACHIEVE MY WEEKLY GOAL:

_____

_____

_____

MONTH ___/ _____

WRAP THIS BABY UP.

41

MY MARKETING FOCUS FOR TODAY IS:

_____

_____

TODAY'S 3 ACTION STEPS TO ACHIEVE MY WEEKLY GOAL:

_____

_____

_____

MONTH ___/ _____

REFLECT & REWARD

42

MY MARKETING FOCUS FOR TODAY IS:

_____

_____

TODAY'S 3 ACTION STEPS TO ACHIEVE MY WEEKLY GOAL:

_____

_____

_____

almost half-way
CHECK IN

We've made it almost half-way through your journey! How are you doing? Are you hanging in there?

Stay the course!

Here's a great featured author story to help you and encourage you as you imagine the possibilities if you stay focused and stay on track.

-

STAY FOCUSED; KEEP PUSHING THE LIMITS

melissa storm

NY TIMES BESTSELLING AUTHOR & BOOK MARKETING EXPERT

Melissa Storm is a New York Times and multiple USA Today bestselling author of Women's Fiction, Inspirational Romance, and Cozy Mysteries. She loves books so much, in fact, that she married fellow author Falcon Storm. Between the two of them, there are always plenty of imaginative, awe-inspiring stories to share. Melissa and Falcon also run a number of book-related businesses together, including LitRing, Sweet Promise Press, Novel Publicity, Your Author Engine, and the Author Site. When she's not reading, writing, or child-rearing, Melissa spends time relaxing at her home in the Michigan woods, where she is kept company by a seemingly unending quantity of dogs and two very demanding Maine Coon rescues. She also writes under the names of Molly Fitz and Mila Riggs.

Everything you do in life, every choice you make, either creates connection or drives disconnection.

www.facebook.com/MelStormAuthor
https://www.instagram.com/melstormauthor/

WORDS OF WISDOM
MEL STORM

Genre: Fiction (Sweet, Cozy, and Sweet Paranormal)

Focus is so critical for authors trying to grow their author brand and sell more books. If I had to do it all over again, I wouldn't chase all those shiny, new ideas so often. A lot of the work I had to do to really get my career moving was all about refocusing my brand and getting things back into nice, neat, little boxes. Do it first or do it best (rather than trying to do it all). Seriously, I say it all the time!

STAY FOCUSED

Mel had a lot of things going on with her career at one time. She admits her biggest struggle was probably her success as a marketer. She started my author career right around the same time she started her company, Novel Publicity and her success with that company as a book marketer for other authors pretty much overshadowed any attempts she had to really push her own author brand.

Eventually she learned how to write in different genres and brand herself under pen names in each of those genres, once again, so that she wouldn't confuse her readers. She writes sweet women's fiction as Melissa Storm, cozy mysteries as Molly Fitz, and most recently, Sweet Paranormal as the co-author pen name Mila Riggs.

2017 was the year when things really started to take off for Mel. She hired my virtual assistant, Angi, who has proven to be an integral part of all of her businesses, and then continued to build my team with smart, trustworthy people. She'd been doing everything herself for far too long and realized that if she was going to focus on her writing and book marketing, she needed help. By delegating, she was finally able to start giving my writing career the same TLC I'd always given her marketing one.

And it paid off! Mel says, "That was also the year I first made the USA Today bestseller list and that Amazon offered me a Kindle Worlds series based on my First Street Church series."

That is also the year she started the Your Author Engine courses to help authors with their marketing efforts.

You can learn all about everything Mel is up to here:

Melissa Storm - melstorm.com
Molly Fitz - https://mollymysteries.com/
Mila Riggs - https://milariggs.com/

Week 7: Day 43

SUNDAY, WEEK OF __ / __ / __

Set aside at least 20 minutes each Monday to set yourself up for the week ahead. Refer back to the weekly goals and fill them in your first weeks goal here. Specifically, when will you be marketing?

My goal for the week is:

_____

_____

_____

What do I need to do before I can move forward with this goal?

_____

_____

_____

On a scale of 1-10, how committed am I to achieving this one goal this week?

1 2 3 4 5 6 7 8 9 10

What am I most proud of for accomplishing so far?

_____

_____

_____

44

MONTH _____/_____

I CAN TOTALLY SMASH THIS.

MY MARKETING FOCUS FOR TODAY IS:

_____

_____

TODAY'S 3 ACTION STEPS TO ACHIEVE MY WEEKLY GOAL:

_____

_____

_____

45

MONTH _____/_____

I'M GONNA WIN OVER THIS.

MY MARKETING FOCUS FOR TODAY IS:

_____

_____

TODAY'S 3 ACTION STEPS TO ACHIEVE MY WEEKLY GOAL:

_____

_____

_____

46

MONTH _____/____
THIS IS WHAT I'M DOING.

MY MARKETING FOCUS FOR TODAY IS:

_____

_____

TODAY'S 3 ACTION STEPS TO ACHIEVE MY WEEKLY GOAL:

_____

_____

47

MONTH _____/____
IT'S OK TO CATCH UP IF I GET BEHIND.

MY MARKETING FOCUS FOR TODAY IS:

_____

_____

TODAY'S 3 ACTION STEPS TO ACHIEVE MY WEEKLY GOAL:

_____

_____

_____

MONTH ____ / _____ **48**

MY MARKETING FOCUS FOR TODAY IS:

_____

_____

TODAY'S 3 ACTION STEPS TO ACHIEVE MY WEEKLY GOAL:

_____

_____

_____

MONTH ____ / _____ **49**

REFLECT & REWARD

MY MARKETING FOCUS FOR TODAY IS:

_____

_____

TODAY'S 3 ACTION STEPS TO ACHIEVE MY WEEKLY GOAL:

_____

_____

_____

Week 8: Day 50

SUNDAY, WEEK OF __ / __ / __

Set aside at least 20 minutes each Monday to set yourself up for the week ahead. Refer back to the weekly goals and fill them in your first weeks goal here. Specifically, when will you be marketing?

My goal for the week is:

_____

_____

_____

What do I need to do before I can move forward with this goal?

_____

_____

_____

On a scale of 1-10, how committed am I to achieving this one goal this week?

1 2 3 4 5 6 7 8 9 10

What am I most proud of for accomplishing so far?

_____

_____

_____

MONTH _____ / _____

I CAN TOTALLY SMASH THIS.

51

MY MARKETING FOCUS FOR TODAY IS:

_____

_____

TODAY'S 3 ACTION STEPS TO ACHIEVE MY WEEKLY GOAL:

_____

_____

_____

MONTH _____ / _____

I'M GONNA WIN OVER THIS.

52

MY MARKETING FOCUS FOR TODAY IS:

_____

_____

TODAY'S 3 ACTION STEPS TO ACHIEVE MY WEEKLY GOAL:

_____

_____

_____

53

MONTH_____/_

THIS IS WHAT I'M DOING.

MY MARKETING FOCUS FOR TODAY IS:

_____

_____

TODAY'S 3 ACTION STEPS TO ACHIEVE MY WEEKLY GOAL:

_____

_____

_____

54

MONTH_____/_____

IT'S OK TO CATCH UP IF I GET BEHIND.

MY MARKETING FOCUS FOR TODAY IS:

_____

_____

TODAY'S 3 ACTION STEPS TO ACHIEVE MY WEEKLY GOAL:

_____

_____

_____

MONTH ____ / _____
WRAP THIS BABY UP.

MY MARKETING FOCUS FOR TODAY IS:

_____

_____

TODAY'S 3 ACTION STEPS TO ACHIEVE MY WEEKLY GOAL:

_____

_____

_____

MONTH ____ / _____
REFLECT & REWARD

MY MARKETING FOCUS FOR TODAY IS:

_____

_____

TODAY'S 3 ACTION STEPS TO ACHIEVE MY WEEKLY GOAL:

_____

_____

_____

Week 9: Day 57
SUNDAY, WEEK OF __ / __ / __

Set aside at least 20 minutes each Monday to set yourself up for the week ahead. Refer back to the weekly goals and fill them in your first weeks goal here. Specifically, when will you be marketing?

My goal for the week is:

_____

_____

_____

What do I need to do before I can move forward with this goal?

_____

_____

_____

On a scale of 1-10, how committed am I to achieving this one goal this week?

1 2 3 4 5 6 7 8 9 10

What am I most proud of for accomplishing so far?

_____

_____

_____

MONTH ___/ _____   **58**
CAN TOTALLY SMASH THIS.

MY MARKETING FOCUS FOR TODAY IS:

_____

_____

TODAY'S 3 ACTION STEPS TO ACHIEVE MY WEEKLY GOAL:

_____

_____

_____

MONTH ___/ _____   **59**
I'M GONNA WIN OVER THIS.

MY MARKETING FOCUS FOR TODAY IS:

_____

_____

TODAY'S 3 ACTION STEPS TO ACHIEVE MY WEEKLY GOAL:

_____

_____

_____

60

MONTH _____/____
THIS IS WHAT I'M DOING.

MY MARKETING FOCUS FOR TODAY IS:

_____

_____

TODAY'S 3 ACTION STEPS TO ACHIEVE MY WEEKLY GOAL:

_____

_____

_____

61

MONTH_____/____
IT'S OK TO CATCH UP IF I GET BEHIND.

MY MARKETING FOCUS FOR TODAY IS:

_____

_____

TODAY'S 3 ACTION STEPS TO ACHIEVE MY WEEKLY GOAL:

_____

_____

_____

MONTH ___ / _____

WRAP THIS BABY UP.

62

MY MARKETING FOCUS FOR TODAY IS:

_____

_____

TODAY'S 3 ACTION STEPS TO ACHIEVE MY WEEKLY GOAL:

_____

_____

_____

MONTH ___ / _____

REFLECT & REWARD

63

MY MARKETING FOCUS FOR TODAY IS:

_____

_____

TODAY'S 3 ACTION STEPS TO ACHIEVE MY WEEKLY GOAL:

_____

_____

_____

Week 10: Day 64

SUNDAY, WEEK OF __ / __ / __

Set aside at least 20 minutes each Monday to set yourself up for the week ahead. Refer back to the weekly goals and fill them in your first weeks goal here. Specifically, when will you be marketing?

My goal for the week is:

_____

_____

_____

What do I need to do before I can move forward with this goal?

_____

_____

_____

On a scale of 1-10, how committed am I to achieving this one goal this week?

1 2 3 4 5 6 7 8 9 10

What am I most proud of for accomplishing so far?

_____

_____

_____

MONTH ___ / _____
CAN TOTALLY SMASH THIS.

MY MARKETING FOCUS FOR TODAY IS:

_____

_____

TODAY'S 3 ACTION STEPS TO ACHIEVE MY WEEKLY GOAL:

_____

_____

_____

MONTH ___ / _____
I'M GONNA WIN OVER THIS

MY MARKETING FOCUS FOR TODAY IS:

_____

_____

TODAY'S 3 ACTION STEPS TO ACHIEVE MY WEEKLY GOAL:

_____

_____

_____

67

MONTH _____ / ____
THIS IS WHAT I'M DOING.

MY MARKETING FOCUS FOR TODAY IS:

_____

_____

TODAY'S 3 ACTION STEPS TO ACHIEVE MY WEEKLY GOAL:

_____

_____

_____

68

MONTH _____ / ____
IT'S OK TO CATCH UP IF I GET BEHIND.

MY MARKETING FOCUS FOR TODAY IS:

_____

_____

TODAY'S 3 ACTION STEPS TO ACHIEVE MY WEEKLY GOAL:

_____

_____

_____

MONTH ___/ _____
WRAP THIS BABY UP.

MY MARKETING FOCUS FOR TODAY IS:

_____

_____

TODAY'S 3 ACTION STEPS TO ACHIEVE MY WEEKLY GOAL:

_____

_____

_____

MONTH ___/ _____
REFLECT & REWARD

MY MARKETING FOCUS FOR TODAY IS:

_____

_____

TODAY'S 3 ACTION STEPS TO ACHIEVE MY WEEKLY GOAL:

_____

_____

_____

Week 11: Day 71
SUNDAY, WEEK OF _ _ / _ _ / _ _

Set aside at least 20 minutes each Monday to set yourself up for the week ahead. Refer back to the weekly goals and fill them in your first weeks goal here. Specifically, when will you be marketing?

My goal for the week is:

_____

_____

_____

What do I need to do before I can move forward with this goal?

_____

_____

_____

On a scale of 1-10, how committed am I to achieving this one goal this week?

1 2 3 4 5 6 7 8 9 10

What am I most proud of for accomplishing so far?

_____

_____

_____

72

MONTH ____ / _____
CAN TOTALLY SMASH THIS.

MY MARKETING FOCUS FOR TODAY IS:

_____

_____

TODAY'S 3 ACTION STEPS TO ACHIEVE MY WEEKLY GOAL:

_____

_____

_____

73

MONTH ____ / _____
I'M GONNA WIN OVER THIS

MY MARKETING FOCUS FOR TODAY IS:

_____

_____

TODAY'S 3 ACTION STEPS TO ACHIEVE MY WEEKLY GOAL:

_____

_____

_____

74

MONTH _____/____
THIS IS WHAT I'M DOING.

MY MARKETING FOCUS FOR TODAY IS:

_____

_____

TODAY'S 3 ACTION STEPS TO ACHIEVE MY WEEKLY GOAL:

_____

_____

_____

75

MONTH_____/____
IT'S OK TO CATCH UP IF I GET BEHIND.

MY MARKETING FOCUS FOR TODAY IS:

_____

_____

TODAY'S 3 ACTION STEPS TO ACHIEVE MY WEEKLY GOAL:

_____

_____

_____

76

MONTH ___ / _____
WRAP THIS BABY UP.

MY MARKETING FOCUS FOR TODAY IS:

_____

_____

TODAY'S 3 ACTION STEPS TO ACHIEVE MY WEEKLY GOAL:

_____

_____

_____

77

MONTH ___ / _____
REFLECT & REWARD

MY MARKETING FOCUS FOR TODAY IS:

_____

_____

TODAY'S 3 ACTION STEPS TO ACHIEVE MY WEEKLY GOAL:

_____

_____

_____

Week 12: Day 78
SUNDAY, WEEK OF _ _ / _ _ / _ _

Set aside at least 20 minutes each Monday to set yourself up for the week ahead. Refer back to the weekly goals and fill them in your first weeks goal here. Specifically, when will you be marketing?

My goal for the week is:

_____

_____

_____

What do I need to do before I can move forward with this goal?

_____

_____

_____

On a scale of 1-10, how committed am I to achieving this one goal this week?

1 2 3 4 5 6 7 8 9 10

What am I most proud of for accomplishing so far?

_____

_____

_____

79

MONTH _____ / _____
CAN TOTALLY SMASH THIS.

MY MARKETING FOCUS FOR TODAY IS:

_____

_____

TODAY'S 3 ACTION STEPS TO ACHIEVE MY WEEKLY GOAL:

_____

_____

_____

80

MONTH ___ / _____
I'M GONNA WIN OVER THIS

MY MARKETING FOCUS FOR TODAY IS:

_____

_____

TODAY'S 3 ACTION STEPS TO ACHIEVE MY WEEKLY GOAL:

_____

_____

_____

81

MONTH _____/____
THIS IS WHAT I'M DOING.

MY MARKETING FOCUS FOR TODAY IS:

_____

_____

TODAY'S 3 ACTION STEPS TO ACHIEVE MY WEEKLY GOAL:

_____

_____

_____

82

MONTH_____/____
IT'S OK TO CATCH UP IF I GET BEHIND.

MY MARKETING FOCUS FOR TODAY IS:

_____

_____

TODAY'S 3 ACTION STEPS TO ACHIEVE MY WEEKLY GOAL:

_____

_____

_____

MONTH _____ / _____

83

WRAP THIS BABY UP.

MY MARKETING FOCUS FOR TODAY IS:

_____

_____

TODAY'S 3 ACTION STEPS TO ACHIEVE MY WEEKLY GOAL:

_____

_____

_____

MONTH _____ / _____

84

REFLECT & REWARD

MY MARKETING FOCUS FOR TODAY IS:

_____

_____

TODAY'S 3 ACTION STEPS TO ACHIEVE MY WEEKLY GOAL:

_____

_____

_____

Think Outside the Box for Marketing!

shelly longenecker

ENTREPRENEUR & AUTHOR

Shelly is a wife, mother of 4, and author. When her son was diagnosed 10 years ago with several food allergies, she felt completely overwhelmed, believing the myth that she had to spend a fortune on food and all day in the kitchen to feed her family safe, whole foods. She couldn't find anything on the market that taught her how to eat a frugal, simple, allergy-friendly whole food, veggie-forward diet, so she created her own system that ticked all these boxes and turned it into a book to share with you. Shelly is the founder and author of Dinner for a Dollar where she explains how she feeds her family a simple, allergy-friendly, whole food diet with loads of fruits and veggies for $1 per person per meal.

"The results your craving are in the work you're avoiding"
Krista Lockwood.

www.facebook.com/dinnerforadollar
http://instagram.com/dinnerforadollar

I consider myself more of an entrepreneur than an author. I use writing as a part of my overall marketing plan. I constantly look for smart business opportunities to get my book in front of new audiences. Especially if you're willing to consider joint ventures with other business owners and affiliate relationships.

THERE ARE SO MANY OPPORTUNITIES...

Shelly shared that she discovered 2 effective strategies that double as additional income streams and as a way to grow her audience.

One is partnering with complementary businesses in affiliate relationships. The other is hosting Book Clubs. For those who are new to affiliate marketing, in this case it's when someone else promotes your book or product in exchange for a cut of the profit.

So far, Shelly has created 3 affiliate partnerships. Shelly shared her three important strategies to make it work.

1. For the relationship to be successful, it has to be a win-win-win. Me partnering with their existing model has to be a win for me, for the other business owner, and for the audience. This seems obvious, but its easy to overlook. You can't just come into someone else's audience and sell your book. That doesn't really work (I've tried). The audience must have a need they want to meet that the other business owner cant/wont/doesn't want to meet that you CAN meet. When you find this type of relationship, it can be a powerful partnership.

2. Look for affiliate partnerships who have the same target market as you, but are operating in a different niche.

My niche is frugal, fast whole food. Complementary relationships for me are groups with my same target market (healthy minded moms with kids at home) but different areas of focus - like general mom groups, minimalist groups, specialty diet groups that need to save $, medical condition tyo groups that benefit from a whole food plant forward diet, budget groups, fitness groups, homeschool groups. You get the idea.

3. Look for affiliate relationships in groups where the audience is growing, engaged, and listening to their leader. If the group isn't doing all of those 3 things, don't partner with them.

As with everything else related to marketing, creating strong and effective affiliate relationships takes time and attention. Especially for the authors that are trying to grow a brand, not just sell some books.

Shelly has also had success with hosting Book Clubs. Shelly likes to host book clubs because they:

a) insert cash flow into her business

b) cost very little to produce (unlike a course)

c) can be developed and adapted as you go (so the time investment is spread out)

d) be recorded to use in the future for evergreen content (so the income from the book club serves as the seed money to create and asset)

e) allows her to interact meaningfully and deeply with her readers - helping them create lasting change (and thereby becoming brand ambassadors).

Using book clubs and affiliate relationships has kept a stream of additional income coming and her schedule full, as she is continually being introduced to new readers through these partnerships.

Learn more about Shelly at www.dinnerforadollar.co.

"Marketing is first and foremost about connecting."

Wendy Paine Miller

Week 13: Day 85
SUNDAY, WEEK OF __ / __ / __

You made it to the FINAL WEEK! For this round! Now marketing should be a part of your author fiber!! Keep working hard, don't stop just because the journal did.

Set aside at least 20 minutes each Monday to set yourself up for the week ahead. Refer back to the weekly goals and fill them in your first weeks goal here. Specifically, when will you be marketing?

My goal for the week is:

_____

_____

_____

What do I need to do before I can move forward with this goal?

_____

_____

_____

On a scale of 1-10, how committed am I to achieving this one goal this week?

1 2 3 4 5 6 7 8 9 10

What am I most proud of for accomplishing so far?

_____

_____

_____

MONTH ____/ _____ **86**
CAN TOTALLY SMASH THIS.

MY MARKETING FOCUS FOR TODAY IS:

_____

_____

TODAY'S 3 ACTION STEPS TO ACHIEVE MY WEEKLY GOAL:

_____

_____

_____

MONTH ____/ _____ **87**
I'M GONNA WIN OVER THIS

MY MARKETING FOCUS FOR TODAY IS:

_____

_____

TODAY'S 3 ACTION STEPS TO ACHIEVE MY WEEKLY GOAL:

_____

_____

_____

88

MONTH _____/ ____
THIS IS WHAT I'M DOING.

MY MARKETING FOCUS FOR TODAY IS:

_____

_____

TODAY'S 3 ACTION STEPS TO ACHIEVE MY WEEKLY GOAL:

_____

_____

_____

89

MONTH _____/ ____
IT'S OK TO CATCH UP IF I GET BEHIND.

MY MARKETING FOCUS FOR TODAY IS:

_____

_____

TODAY'S 3 ACTION STEPS TO ACHIEVE MY WEEKLY GOAL:

_____

_____

_____

MONTH ___/ _____

MY MARKETING FOCUS FOR TODAY IS:

_____

_____

TODAY'S 3 ACTION STEPS TO ACHIEVE MY WEEKLY GOAL:

_____

_____

_____

rocked that!

NOW THAT'SHOW IT'S DONE.

DID I ACHIEVE MY GOAL?

_____

_____

WHAT WILL I START WORKING TOWARD NEXT?

_____

_____

_____

NOW WHAT?

Congratulations on making it through the journal!

By the end of 90 days, hopefully you've made some great progress in your book. Don't forget to check out the extra resources for you to use at https://writepublishsell.com/JMI-secret. PW: JMIrocks (case sensitive).

This book will teach you the first set of skills to effectively build your longterm marketing strategy on a solid foundation. When it's time to incorporate more advanced strategeis, you may need more training and support, or even prefer to hire people to help you out.

We have some additional support and extra resources that speak to those needs on the website too, and of course, we offer services and consulting should you be interested at some point.

I'm so excited that you've started this journey and I cannot wait to see how it goes for you! Please keep me posted! Join us in the Write|Publish|Sell Facebook group for additional support. (https://facebook.com/groups/writepublishsell)

With Love and BEST wishes for marketing success,

Alexa

THANK YOU

The journal you're holding in your hands is one of the tools in the *Write|Publish|Sell* program suite of courses, training, coaching, and publishing support. I want to say a big thanks to all the people without who helped me bring it to life.

Thank you Neesha Mirchandani for the big brainstorming that led to the first book in this series. Thank you for creating the plug- and-play Quick Wins Productivity System by Impact Stars, LLC, which is what led to the creation of this series. Thank you especially for connecting me with Cindy Tyler and Vervante Press. Cindy continues to be a massive mentor, supporter, and all-around amazing woman in my life.

Michelle, your cover design skills and graphics work never cease to amaze me!

Nancy, Raewyn, Sarah, and Emily: I couldn't ever ask for a better team in running this business. Thank you, truly, for all you do. You are all so very appreciated.

Thank you especially to all of the authors who bravely contributed their stories, fears, and marketing successes and challenges. You made this book a real pleasure to write. I'm so glad that most of you have become good friends and colleagues and I'm excited to watch your continued successes.

Braedan, Ella, and Charis... thank you for your continued sacrifice, in ways you may not even understand yet, so that your mom can continue to follow her dreams. You three mean everything to me.

Ideas and Notes

ALEXA BIGWARFE – AUTHOR

Alexa Bigwarfe is a mother to 3 wildlings, author, publisher, writer-entrepreneur, and podcaster. Her writing career began after her infant daughter passed away at 2 days old. She has written and/ or edited and self-published numerous books of her own and shephereded/assisted in the publishing and book launch process for hundreds of other authors through her company Write|Publish|Sell. She uses that hard-earned publishing knowledge to support other writers and connect them to resources for completing, publishing, and marketing their books through the annual Women in Publishing Summit, a free online conference which takes place in March. Join her free group about writing, publishing, and selling at http://facebook.com/ groups/WritePublishSell.

www.writepublishsell.com
www.womeninpublishingsummit.com

Printed in Great Britain
by Amazon

43684101R00127